Low Carb Vegan Cooking
Quick and Simple Recipes for Everyday Meals

1st Edition

Mike Ludo, PhD

ISBN: 978-1-998174-02-7
Plant Slant Press
Vancouver, BC, Canada, 2023

Introduction

A plant-based diet is the best thing you can do simultaneously for both your body and the planet. Animal agriculture produces more greenhouse gasses than all sectors of transportation combined, so you will be doing more than your part to address a changing climate by switching to a plant-based diet. And keeping animal products out of your bloodstream not only reduces your chances of developing a wide range of lifestyle-related diseases (ranging from diabetes to cardiovascular disease, obesity and dementia), but has also been shown in research to have effects of reversing conditions associated with previous years' habits of eating meat, eggs and dairy. Even if you've spent the first 50 years of your life eating cheeseburgers and drinking milk shakes, eating plant-based meals will allow your body's healing systems to get to work undoing many previous years of unhealthy eating.

This book is designed to serve a range of dietary goals, including Weight Loss, Weight Maintenance, Caloric Restriction and Practical Veganism. I draw on a range of inspirations from the world's cuisines, including European, Asian (East and South), North American, Middle Eastern, African and Latin American traditions. The recipes are generally compatible with other low carb diets such as Keto and South Beach, but there are some differences. I have not found the keto ethos of "just replace carbs with a lot of fat" to be particularly useful. For one, many keto recipes call for high amounts of saturated fats, usually derived from coconut-based oils and fats. The main source of coconut-derived fats in this book are with vegan cheeses, so simply skip the cheese, or reduce the amount, if coconut fat concerns you. I certainly wouldn't advise eating vegan cheese every day, but as a cheat meal once a week or so is something I personally am comfortable with, based on the results of my bloodwork.

I think of it this way—the body is at homeostasis around 98.6 degrees Fahrenheit or 37 degrees Celsius. If you've ever bought a container of coconut oil, you know that its contents are liquid in the heat of summer, whereas the fat on a steak at the same summer temperature is still solid. I use that difference as a visual metaphor for what I want in my veins and arteries. This is not quite scientific, of course, but I feel better imagining coconut fats in my blood circulating as liquids in the warm medium of my body, and I imagine animal fats wanting to congeal into solid blobs and I definitely don't want that! Also, if your goal is weight loss, adding lots of calories in your diet through high amounts of fat won't really help you achieve your goals (this is where I part ways with the keto ethos), especially since fat is harder to metabolize than carbs and often just gets added to your already-existing fat stores.

All that being said, the recipes in this book are broadly compatible with keto diets, depending on how you tweak portion sizes and ingredient amounts. The recipes are also compatible with South Beach though skew closer towards Phase 1 of that diet, which has 3 phases in which one gradually increases the carb intake (Phase 1 has the least carbs, while Phase 3 has the most). Again, you can tweak recipes in their portion sizes and ingredient amounts to traverse the phase spectrum of South Beach, if those are guidelines you are following.

The book's recipes support a practice of caloric restriction, which has been associated in research with a wide range of positive benefits for health such as increased lifespan, better metabolism, weight management, cardiovascular health, cellular repair and maintenance, cognitive benefits and cancer risk reduction. A low carb diet can be thought of as a convenient shortcut to reduce the overall intake of calories, provided you do not just replace carbs with a lot of fat.

This book is *not* about showcasing difficult gourmet recipes for experienced epicures with massive kitchens or for those wanting to impress friends at dinner parties, though I must say, my friends have been impressed by how amazing many of these meals taste, and you are allowed to party with this food all you like! It's just not the goal of this particular volume to focus on recipes that require a lot of work, cost and planning since the focus is on everyday meals that anyone can easily make.

I have aimed for describing meals that are simple and relatively fast to prepare. I would even say that most of the recipes are for lazy people, because I consider myself to be a lazy cook—usually I want to get cooking done quickly so I can do other things with my day. But not too quickly in the manner of fast food habits. Instead, I try to cultivate a certain amount of mindfulness in my cooking practices so that I pay attention to what I am doing and devote a reasonable amount of a day's time to making my meals. While at first glance some of the recipes may not seem to be so 'fast and simple," because many of them can be made in large batches, the time per serving makes them very fast on average, so if you'd like each serving to take less time to make, just make more of the dish at once. I also don't focus too much on presentation, by making the food look as pretty as possible, as you will see from the straightforward cell phone camera photos of the food on the companion blog (medium.com/low-carb-vegan). That being said, I do think the food looks pretty enough :)

Most of the recipes are not particularly hard on the wallet, but if you find yourself gravitating towards a lot of vegan meat and cheese substitutes, those will obviously cost more compared to buying raw vegetables in the produce section, since a lot of lab research, processing, packaging and marketing goes into making a reasonable stand-in for mozzarella, hamburger patty or ground chorizo that you find at your local sustainable organic organic grocer. This book includes some recipes that feature these more expensive ingredients but they are not the focus of the meals presented here overall. In general, a vegan diet is less expensive compared to a diet that includes animal products since meat and dairy are relatively expensive, and the more you want imitation meat and dairy in your diet, or even premade vegan kimchi, you will have to be prepared to pay for it unless you start making it yourself. Making such ingredients from scratch goes a bit beyond the 'fast and easy' concept in this book's title, and so may be a topic for another volume from me, or some web searching from you.

I am a Doctor, But...

While I have a PhD, my research was in interdisciplinary technology design, not in health, medicine or nutrition. Nothing in this volume should be construed as professional advice in these areas of specialist expertise. While I have done a lot of my own academic journal reading on topics related to the overall nutritional approach of these recipes using my general PhD skills, the recipes in this volume are derived primarily from my everyday eating habits based on my own history of personal goals around weight loss, weight maintenance, caloric restriction and practical veganism.

If you are interested in gluten free eating, you will find plenty here that does not contain gluten. If you are allergic to nuts, please don't eat them even if my recipe includes them. Ultimately, you are responsible for what you eat, and I am just sharing my own opinions and experiences in these pages. If you have health concerns about a low carb vegan diet, please consult with your own doctor because I am certainly not that kind of doctor, and I do not pretend to be. I have turned my kitchen into an informal food lab, and this book is an output of that personal research of mine.

Where are the Photos of The Food?

To make this book as affordable as possible, I have omitted images throughout since images add cost to book production. Instead, I have placed all the food photos all on the companion blog, medium.com/low-carb-vegan. Online, you can view well-organized full color photos of all the food discussed in the book, organized by topic section.

Recipe Approach

Because of this book's strong focus on practical everyday veganism, I have largely omitted traditional cookbook items such as exact measurements for ingredients, quantified portion sizes or nutritional estimates of the final prepared meal. There are many good reasons for this. For one, your mileage may vary based on the exact brand of some item you purchase, or the type and size of your cooking ware (e.g. the amount of oil you may use to stir fry konjac rice will be related to the kind of metal and the size and shape of your pan or wok), or your personal tastes and goals. Like many if not most people, I usually find serving sizes to be ludicrously or unrealistically small, and when eating the kind of food described in this book, it is pretty hard to gain weight, unless

you start consuming whole bricks of vegan cheese or drinking
bottles of olive oil (please don't!).

Another reason is that your goals may vary. A good vegan chorizo
will have some carbs and fat in it. If your goal is weight loss, you
should use a small amount of this tasty stuff and treat it mainly as
a way to add some interest and flavor to your konjac rice or pasta
(or in my kimchi tofu soup). But if you are looking just to maintain
weight and aren't as focused on shedding some excess pounds, by
all means add in more vegan ground chorizo and "live a little." The
same goes with other ingredients, such as ratios of fruit-infused
balsamic vinegar to infused olive oil, or even just the amount of oil
to use. Or, my blender may be smaller or larger than yours, so you
will have to adjust for what makes sense for your kitchen tools. For
purposes of caloric restriction, when it comes to non-dairy milks, I
will usually recommend unsweetened almond or soy milk but if
you don't mind the extra calories, feel free to use oat milk instead
because hey, it tastes a lot better (!) because of the sugars.

In other words, the recipes should be treated as guidelines, not as
strict rule sets like an algorithm. In computer science, definitions
of what an algorithm is usually say something like: "it's how you
tell the computer what to do, like following a recipe, do these
steps in this sequence by these amounts" etc. My recipes provide
you with enough structure as to what is supposed to be
accomplished, and the full color photos on my blog give you an
idea of what the end result might look like. My recipes also feature
suggestions for variations so that you understand the general
principles behind my approach.

Because the recipes are simple, they are easy to modify to your
own tastes, and that is intentional. Have you ever noticed that
every sushi restaurant seems to have the same menu? Or every
pub? Or every steakhouse? With food culture, there are always
strong business pressures to gravitate towards the center
statistical trend line or lowest common denominator or most
average taste of the greatest number of people. The recipes in this
book are not aimed to please the largest population possible.
Instead, I have provided a wide variety of food to try and if you
don't like hot spices, for example, just don't use them, or if you
don't like peeling apart and washing the leaves of fresh herbs, just
sprinkle in the dried kind instead. Use the recipes as a platform to

create variations that are closer to what you usually like to eat or for the kind of attention and care you want to bring to your cooking. This is easy to do, because the recipes themselves are pretty easy.

Humor Warning

Throughout the book, I periodically use humor—that's because I do sit down comedy on the side and to be funny, one has to keep practicing being funny, or at least trying to be. The humor has a number of useful functions in the recipes. Often, I am just trying to get you to think about cooking more creatively, less as something to get through to accomplish a goal—like eating the resulting food and stocking the fridge with leftovers—and more as a creative activity for play and experimentation.

A good joke is also memorable and so the food will lodge into your short term memory longer if you laugh, since emotional responses help a lot with learning in general. I also want to get away from the Michelin chef star vibe of so many cookbooks, and keep this kind of cooking as everyday and down to earth as possible, so I need to occasionally debunk my own pretentious seriousness that may creep into the recipes. I suppose I may also want to sometimes entertain the reader, too! You will likely find some of the jokes to be total groaners, but some will probably make you smile a bit, so just bear with me as I try to humor you sometimes.

Fueling Workouts

Using just my person for empirical human subject research, I can attest that the kinds of meals you can put together out of these recipes will support exercise, despite their low carb count. Exercise, of course, requires fuel, typically carbs, for the body to burn in order to produce work. Some research I've read suggests that fasted cardio workouts burn more calories during the workout, but properly carb-fueled workouts continue to burn more calories after the workout. So, this may turn out to be a difference that just doesn't make much of a difference, other than how you personally prefer to work out. I don't like the feeling of working out without energy, and so am not a fan of fasted cardio exercising, despite its current popularity with Hollywood personal trainers who are very good at turning out comic book superhero bodies in their cinematic version.

I've found that with these low carb vegan meals, I can easily do resistance training, for instance a full-body workout for 90-120 minutes, or a half hour on an elliptical training (or equivalent shorter duration sprint training on similar equipment) even after resistance training. These meals can also easily fuel hot yoga for 60-90 minutes or a bike ride to a craft brewery 20 miles (32 km) away from my home.

What these meals do *not* fuel well is cycling or hiking for many hours, for which I have two solutions: pack into your bag either 1-3 (depending on how long your hike or ride is and how big your bag and root veggies are) boiled sweet potatoes or baked Japanese purple yams. This cookbook avoids overly processed foods such as typical energy or power bars that are marketed heavily to runners and cyclists. Eat those dense pricey factory mass produced rectangular things if you want, but I've found that nutrient-rich varieties of potatoes do the job for fueling long hours of more intense cycling or long distance hiking very effectively (here in the Vancouver area, it's not unusual to casually decide to go on a 20km hike on a whim, with the dog of course!).

I can't comment too much on how this diet relates to folks who want to really bulk up from lifting weights. With this diet I have both lost weight (from shedding fat) and increased muscle mass from resistance training, at the same time, but not at Hemsworth or Cavill (superhero dude) levels. My understanding is that to build lots of muscle mass, you need to eat a *lot* of calories, which goes against the low-carb caloric restriction approach in this book.

For a superhero or professional body builder body, there is usually a bulking up phase through high calorie consumption, which includes adding a lot of fat to your body so that you can achieve appropriate levels of protein synthesis needed for increased lot of muscle size, which is followed by a slimming down phase, where you shed the fat to reveal the muscle. And in professional practice, taking steroids is common, which is well outside the scope of anything I would write about! I wouldn't recommend the recipes in the book for this kind of professional bulking up weight training, simply because those high calorie counts run counter to the goal of caloric restriction. However, in my experience at least, building muscle mass at more moderate levels is achievable within the dietary constraints of these recipes.

New to Low Carb?

If you're already well experienced with low carb diets, you can skip this section. If going low carb is a new experience for you, the first 2-3 days will likely require some adjustment by your body as it recalibrates to the new energy regime (this duration will likely vary for each individual). My personal experience is that when going into ketosis or just a very low carb metabolic state, I might feel a tad light headed and low energy just for around 2 days, after which I feel fine again. But I also know people who've completely given up on low carb diets because of this initial state of feeling out of energy for a few days.

One of the cool things about a low carb diet is that you are relatively spared typical hunger pangs to a high degree. With a diet that has a medium or high carb load, your blood glucose spikes momentarily, and then comes down again pretty quickly, and this lowering of the glucose levels in your blood (the rate varies depending on what you're eating, e.g. highly processed versus whole foods, but the general principle applies regardless to the exact foods you're consuming) generates a feeling of being hungry again.

With a low carb diet, all this spiking of blood sugar levels (measured by GI or glycemic index, and GL or glycemic load) doesn't happen, and you end up with a more steady state or 'even keel' feeling of energy available. In essence, I don't feel hungry in the same way when on a low carb diet, and the signals the body sends out that a meal is needed are much milder and less pressing compared to a growling stomach!

A missed meal tends not to produce much duress when in a low carb metabolic routine, which is handy since most of the food readily available in social and public spaces tends to be high fat, high carb, animal-based or if plant-based (as with a salad) loaded with sugar in the dressing or fat in the cheese and so on. Being in a low carb metabolic state gives you more time to seek out appropriate foods, and if they are not available, then missing a meal is much easier to deal with compared to a higher carb diet which makes missing a meal a much more miserable experience.

Of course, today a lot of people enjoy Big Pharma solutions like Ozempic, which is another way to free you from hunger. If you find yourself having body weight issues because you feel hungry all the time and are always nibbling on something, you can of course try injecting yourself with some popular profitable drug. Or, just go into a low carb metabolic state, which also is very effective at alleviating regular hunger pangs.

Cheat Days and Meals

This cookbook contains recipes that are very low carb, and some that are just moderately low in carbs. The recipes also range from very low fat to, well, quite a lot of fat! The former are best for weight loss and the latter best for weight maintenance goals. I will point out which recipes have a bit more carbs and fat, so that if your goals are weight loss, you can reserve the higher calorie weight maintenance meals for your cheat days or cheat meals. A cheat day is a whole day of meals when you allow yourself higher calorie meals throughout, whereas a cheat meal is simply one meal in a day that has higher calories than usual. You can also call a day in which you have a cheat meal a cheat day, so I'm a bit flexible with these terms in the book.

My personal recommendation is 1-2 cheat meals per week, spaced out evenly (a few days apart) depending on how often you feel you could use them. So your 'cheat days' are really just a regular day that has one higher-than-normal caloric load meal in the sequence. Cheat meals and days have a number of benefits, such as:

1) Mental relief and the psychological break from constant dietary restrictions.

2) Metabolic boosts: since our bodies adapt to our typical caloric intake, which can make weight loss much harder to achieve, you can thwart over-adaptation by tricking your body into believing that it's not really starving by adding in the occasional higher energy meal. This helps with preventing plateaus whereby your metabolism prevents you from losing weight, by keeping your metabolism responsive and efficient. Note that metabolism is a highly complex bodily-systemic balance that is very difficult to change, despite the tens of thousands of online articles and videos about 'changing your metabolism'--good luck with that! Metabolic shifts are often very temporary. A key hormone involved in regulating hunger and metabolism is leptin, and cheat meals seem to keep leptin on the same side as your personal goals.

3) Allowing cheat meals helps with managing your social life, since usually hanging out with other people for long or more enjoyable periods of time will involve eating and drinking with them. Remember that one of the most common sources of calories is simply being with other people. If you know the gang is going to be eating pizzas and drinking pitchers of beer, maybe minimize your time allotment for that particular gang, or seek out other gangs with healthier habits.

Portion Sizes

This book's focus on practical veganism means doing without standard diet cookbook approaches such as counting calories and carbs, or measuring food weights and portion sizes. All of this micro-measuring isn't very practical, and undermines the book's theme of setting up a dietary regime and routine for easy everyday eating. The recipes of course give appropriate indications of ingredient ratios, tablespoons and grams of course, but let's say you make my seaweed soup—is that 2 or 4 portions? Well, it depends! How large are your bowls? How hungry are you? How many meals or people do you want to spread it across? For me, practical veganism means not micromanaging all the possible quantities one can count. It's hard to gain weight when making balanced and varied meal plans out of the recipes, and very easy to lose or maintain weight with it, so relax and try to go with the kind of casual practical flow that this diet allows for.

A low carb diet vegan done right—by which I mean *practically*, that delivers great nutritional value overall, and that matches your goals of weight loss, weight maintenance or caloric restriction —is one in which you can just eat whatever you want, whenever you want, as much as you want, as long as you are staying within the parameters of the diet paradigm. A good rule of thumb is to eat until you're 80% full (this idea comes from the Blue Zone philosophy of eating for longevity). Keep in mind which meals have more or fewer carbs and fats, and skew towards the former if weight maintenance is your goal and the latter if it is weight loss.

Measurements

If your goals are weight loss, the approach in this book is not so much about measuring grams of carbs and fats or kCals or portion sizes in the recipes. Rather, just *measure yourself*, by every morning stepping on the scale and getting a soft tailor's measuring tape to measure your waistline. Everyday, write those two numbers down in a spreadsheet in adjacent columns (the rows are the days).

Pay attention to those numbers in relation to what you are eating, to develop some mindfulness about the effects of the food you eat on these two measures (weight and waistline). If you want to lose weight and those numbers are not coming down, cut back on the amount of vegan cheese (or skip the meals that have them, or eliminate that one ingredient), and the same goes with vegan meats that are higher in carbs and fat, and which may take you out of ketosis or calorie deficit. Don't eat the chocolate chip muffins for every meal, etc.

Eating and measuring like this in tandem produces amazing insights into how your body interacts with your food. For example, in my case, I simply cannot lose weight while eating the phyllo dough low carb pizzas I describe, but I won't gain weight eating them, either, and so they are better for goals of weight maintenance. Everyone's body is different, and since your weight and waistline are the two 'metrics that matter,' track those two numbers daily against the meals you eat, and you should find the best combination that helps you stay on track with your goals. Once you've reached the desired level of weight loss, since overall the meals in this book are low calorie—especially when compared to what you get in restaurants or the prepared foods in delis and grocery stores—the recipes should work fine for maintaining your new weight.

Expect setbacks, as likely there will be days when the numbers are trending in the wrong direction. If you find yourself putting a bit too much vegan cheese into your pasta or stuffed peppers, skip the cheese, and so on. In the recipes that follow, the main 'guilty parties' when it comes to interfering with weight loss are vegan meats and cheeses, and with a few recipes, melted vegetable margarine or coconut oil. And so, don't eat meals with coconut milk in them everyday. Daily measuring of your weight and waistline will help you sort out which ingredients and meals are friendliest to your weight and calorie goals.

Fruits

Fruits are almost by definition high in sugars and thus are high carb, and so I don't feature them too much in this book. A good cheat meal is a fruit salad, or any collection of fruits you wish to combine. The lowest carb fruits are blackberries, raspberries and strawberries, and apples aren't too bad. Thus, I do include some basic recipes that include these fruits in the book. Also, keep in mind that olives, avocados and tomatoes *are* fruits and these foods do feature prominently in the recipes, so you're not really missing out on this food group if making meal plans out of these recipes for weight loss.

Beans & Legumes

Beans and legumes, like fruits, are very good for you and also high in carbs. Thus, reserve most of this food group for cheat meals. The foods from this family I focus on in the following recipes are soybeans (and the TVP and tofu derived from them), chickpeas (in the form of chickpea flour) and green beans, as these are the lowest carb varieties in this important food category.

Usually one has to combine a bean and a grain to get the amino acids for making complete proteins, such as beans and rice or hummus and pita. Soybeans and tofu offer a complete protein, however, which is why these are emphasized in some of the recipes. And for cheat meals or weight maintenance goals, I include hummus on slices of low carb toast (which have all required amino acids) as in the Toasts section.

Misc Nutrients

There are a few nutrients you need to pay a little extra attention to when on a plant-based diet, which this section discusses.

You may have heard that you can't get vitamin B12 on a vegan diet, but that's not really true. A lot of plant-based foods—such as nutritional yeast, nut and soy milks, cereals, yogurts, and imitation meats—are fortified with essential vitamins including B12, so read your labels. There's also a nutritional yeast spread called Marmite, which basically works in recipes like a salty honey, and it also is fortified with B12 and other vitamins.

You need to have a regular source of iodine, which is easily obtained in iodine-fortified salt. Note that seaweed can be very high in iodine, though, and too much iodine is as bad for you as too little of it, which I discuss more in the seaweed soup recipe, so don't eat seaweed soup for every meal!

Omega-3s can be inefficient for the body to absorb when coming from plant-based sources, which is why the Creamy Green Smoothie recipe contains plenty of ground flax, hemp hearts and chia seeds. Algae-based foods can be better for omega-3 absorption which is why keeping spirulina handy in your pantry is recommended.

Zinc is found in whole grain breads (the low carb variety of course is promoted here), legumes and seeds.

Iron comes in two forms, heme (from animals) and nonheme (from plants). Getting iron from plant-based foods is less efficient (harder for the body to absorb) compared to getting iron from animal products. To increase bodily absorption of nonheme iron, adding vitamin C rich foods and avoiding calcium-rich foods to the meal helps.

Vitamin D comes primarily from sunlight and animal products, both of which can be very harmful! Vitamin D is also found in a lot of fortified vegan foods such as milks, cereals and juices, so I don't recommend many hours of sunbathing because that's a lot of sunscreen and trips to the dermatology test lab indeed!

Getting your blood levels checked regularly is important no matter what your dietary regime is, which will help with spotting any nutritional lacks and imbalances. Taking a vegan dietary multivitamin supplement regularly is a good way to tick off all the nutrient boxes just to make sure nothing is getting missed in the meal routines you set up. My practical veganism approach is to pop a multivitamin supplement daily to minimize the constant counting of nutrients in everything I eat. If you don't like swallowing big pills, I don't either, but the Creamy Green Smoothie makes it pretty easy to swallow pretty much any pill or capsule you wish no matter what size they come in.

Protein

The myth that it's hard to get sufficient protein on a vegan diet has hopefully by now been sufficiently debunked by the popular media. In the richer developed economies, protein deficiency is very rare, and in fact most people consume much more protein than they need. On a vegan diet, one just has to make sure to get enough amino acids from meals that the body can obtain complete protein requirements. The recipes' primary sources of complete proteins are soy (whether in beans, milk, TVP or tofu) and the protein powder supplement for the Creamy Green Smoothie. Seitan is mostly complete, lacking only lysine (and is low on theanine) which can be obtained from seeds and beans in the recipes, or even just the soy from other meals. Theanine is found in tea leaves, and green tea is an important ingredient in the Creamy Green Smoothie. You don't have to get your complete protein in the same meal, since getting them across a day's meals will support your body's protein needs.

Pantry Stocking

Like any cookbook, there are a few categories of items I recommend accumulating for your pantry, with 'pantry' broadly construed to include your fridge and freezer! Basically, you need to keep things around that won't go bad too quickly in the same way as fresh produce, and you don't really want to be running to the store constantly to buy stuff.

Some of the items below will need to be refrigerated after opening, so make clever use of spatial arrangements in your fridge when it comes to managing shelf and drawer space relative to container size—it can be very easy to accumulate quite a lot of ingredients when it comes to any kind of specialized or intentional diet such as a low carb vegan diet. When people say, "OMG, what can you eat?!" just open your fridge and pantry and say, "All this stuff!" And it's a lot of stuff!

Flavor Enhancers

It's a good idea to get to know all of the speciality 'ethnic' delis and groceries in your area, such as those with a focus on Italian, Mediterranean, Middle Eastern, Asian (East and South), Latin American and general European foods and imports. These businesses will provide you with a richer variety of ingredients to add amazing flavors to your cooking. For example, from my local Italian food store, I keep the following in stock:

Capers (I prefer the smaller kind)
Dill and almond pesto (basil pesto is usually loaded with non-vegan cheese particles)
Various olive tapenades
Ajvar (a red pepper spread, the lowest carb version you can find)
Black truffle sauce
Hot sauces (ranging from small expensive bottles that are high on the Scoville scale to massive mild stuff made for the masses)
Various pitted olives (e.g. with pimentos or garlic stuffing, or with no stuffing)
Sun-dried tomatoes

A few blocks away from where I live, there's a Middle Eastern grocer, where I get saffron for my paella, phyllo dough for my pizzas, raw honeycomb and better prices and selection on non-Western typical spices. I also live near Korean, Chinese and Eastern European delis (thank you, Canadian immigration policy!), and as with many cities, there are organic and sustainable supermarkets around.

Judicious use of these flavor enhancers will go a long way towards refining your meal prep and making them, well, very tasty! The thing to watch out for is to not pile them up into the same dish. Read the nutrition label carefully, as you should buy these flavor enhancers with ~1-3 *net carbs* (carbs - fiber = net carbs) per serving. Try to get away with just using one or at most two in a dish, because the more you enhance your meals a lot of these flavors, the fat from the oils and carbs will add up as you load them in, so be strategic and minimalist in your cooking style.

Sweeteners

Keep stevia and monk fruit on hand, ideally both in packet form (for your cups of coffee and tea) and in larger bags more suitable for baking. These are natural non-calorie sweeteners and thus very handy.

Thickeners

Keep bags of guar gum and xanthan gum on hand as thickeners, experiment with both and see which you like best in various applications. A little goes a long way. I actually rarely use them, but sometimes they are just the right trick to make a liquid thick.

Frozen Stuff

Some good things to keep in the freezer are:

Many loaves of sliced low carb bread
Chopped avocados (for the Creamy Green Smoothie)
Kale (also for the Creamy Green Smoothie)
Broccoli florets
Cauliflower florets
Blackberries, raspberries and strawberries
Servings of recipes made in big batches
Prepared veggies

You can see how important the Cream Green Smoothie is to my diet! From this you should take that I drink it daily, because it's a 'super super' food in that it has many ingredients that are each themselves considered to be super foods.

The lowest carb fruits are *blackberries, raspberries* and *strawberries,* so keeping these frozen berries on hand will be good if you ever get a sweet tooth craving that would otherwise send you to the gelato factory.

I also freeze some very choice fancy items like *expensive mushrooms* I sometimes come across in the weekly farmer's market and similar items. For veggies that you won't be eating regularly but also can't come across conveniently, consider washing, slicing and freezing them for easy use in recipes.

Also, some dishes should be made in very large batches so you can freeze servings for easy access later.

Pickled Stuff

Pickled veggies take up a lot of space in the fridge once opened, so I usually buy them at least in pairs, where one jar goes in the fridge and the backup is in the pantry (an exception is kimchi, which is always chilled). My usual collection of jarred pickled veggies include:

Pickles
Mushrooms
Artichokes
Asparagus
Yellow squash
Pitted olives (various kinds)
Kimchi (the vegan variety, available at specialty Asian or organic grocers. Regrettably, mainstream kimchi includes shrimp and fish paste, and equally regrettably, store-bought vegan kimchi costs three or four times as much per volume as the non-vegan kind!).

Spicy Stuff

Online research into the spices with the most amount of scientific research into positive health effects will yield a long list such as:

Basil
Black pepper
Cardamom
Cayenne Pepper
Chili Powder
Clove
Coriander
Cumin
Curry
Dried red pepper
Fennel
Fenugreek

Licorice Root
Nutmeg
Oregano
Parsley
Peppermint
Rosemary
Saffron
Sage
Thyme
Turmeric

Of course, you need to have all of them! In the Super Spice recipe below, I do just that: I literally take all of these spices and make a blend out of them, and then add this summative 'Super Spice' to the dishes that call for them.

Additionally, *cocoa* and *cinnamon* both have health benefits, but these I make into a separate blend for the Smoothed Spiced Coffee (in the Drinks section below).

Fresh Herbs

Most well-stocked grocers sell pre-packaged fresh herbs in the produce section. Keeping a small collection in your fridge of not-dried-out oregano, thyme, dill, mint, basil and other fresh herbs will always come in handy for making your dishes just *explode* with flavor, and I really mean that: Explode! Boom! With flavor!

Omega 3 and 6

Similarly, as I do with the Super Spice, I create a mix of chia seeds, ground flax and hemp hearts, which I store in the fridge as a key ingredient of the Creamy Green Smoothie.

Other Dry Goods

Other dry goods you'll want to keep handy for the recipes in this book include:

Matcha powder
Psyllium husks (fine ground powder form)
A vegan protein powder supplement (for the Creamy Green Smoothie, flavored as you wish)
Spirulina (in its powder form, you can bake with it or blend it into the Creamy Green Smoothie, though it can get quite sticky when wet. You can also take this super food in pill supplement form).
Chickpea flour
Almond flour
Coffee and tea
Nutritional yeast
Baking soda
Baking powder
Black salt (kala namak) for eggy flavor

It's not really a dry good, but some vanilla and other extracts always come in handy.

Convenient Faux Meat and Dairy

When time is of the essence (or when laziness is, that counts, too), it's always handy to have some veggie burger patties (e.g. plant-based imitation meats or the bean and lentil type), or perhaps ground vegan chorizo and sausage links, along with a selection of some of the vegan cheeses (solid or shredded).

Read labels carefully, since typically vegan meats and cheeses are a bit high in either (or both!) carbs and fat, and vegan cheeses especially will be high in fat. These foods are best used for cheat meals or at least very non-regularly, if your goals are weight loss. For weight maintenance, increase frequency of consumption accordingly, if your budget allows. In grad school, we used to call Whole Foods 'Whole Paycheck,' so just remember that these imitation animal products are often as pricey as, well, animal products, if not more so.

Non-dairy milks are a different story, as they are not too expensive (relative to dairy milk) and can be found in unsweetened varieties with negligible fat and carbs while also being heavily fortified with nutritional value.

Bulk Boxed Unsweetened Almond or Soy Milk

For daily low carb vegan dairy style drinking (e.g. coffee and smoothies), the usual best choices are unsweetened (vanilla or plain) almond milk or soy milk, depending on your taste preferences. The kind I use has 1 net gram of carbs per serving, so read the labels and aim for something like that in the brands you choose. Cashew milk tastes (to me) a lot better than almond milk, but the label says it has an additional net gram or so of fat and carbs, so I use it more in dishes and less in drinks.

For practical storing vegan dairy, I recommend unsweetened (plain or vanilla) almond or soy milk that can be stored *unrefrigerated* until opening, since this staple item can take up lots of room if you buy the kind that needs to be refrigerated from the time of purchase. The Creamy Green Smoothie recipe calls for one liter each time it is made, which yields five large glasses that can be stored in the fridge and consumed over a couple days (or in one very hungry day!). I buy the almond milk in bulk boxes of six, and they sit piled up in my garage, next to the bikes.

Flavored Oils and Vinegars

An oil or vinegar is 'infused' if the extra flavors are added afterwards, and 'fused' when produced at the same time. In other words, if you press oranges and olives in one mash to get the oil, you have orange-*fused* extra virgin olive oil, but if you add chipotle chili oil to your olive oil after both are made, then you have a chipotle-*infused* oil. I will just refer to "flavored" oils and vinegars and not worry about whether you obtain fused or infused varieties. For the purposes of your low carb vegan pantry, it's a great idea to get a number of both flavored (white and dark) vinegars and olive oils, because like fresh herbs, they help your dishes *explode* with flavor, and I mean, *explode!*

Konjac

A number of recipes make use of konjac products, which are easy to find in locales that have large Asian supermarkets. If you don't live in such an area, you can also buy these on Amazon or through other online retail sources. Konjac is very low in calories and makes a great substitute for rice, pasta and even cubed potatoes. In the recipes I make use of three kinds of konjac: the noodle form—called shirataki—for pastas, a riced form (so amazing for the paella :) and a solid gelatinous slab (for cubes and slices). Either brown or white konjac varieties will work for the recipes. When store-bought, it is usually chilled and so should be stored in your fridge. If buying online, you can keep it in your pantry until opened (follow the instructions on the package).

A few sources recommend blanching the slab form of konjac prior to using it for cooking, since some people object to its odor right out of the package. What you can do is simply cut a brick in half, and blanch one half of the slab by placing it in boiling water for a few minutes. Remove the blanched konjac slab, and then just do a side-by-side nose comparison against the unblanched slab. Do you think the improvement is worth the blanching step? That will be very subjective. The blanched konjac certainly has less of a konjac smell, but konjac smell doesn't bother me, so 'to blanch or not to blanch' can be treated as a personal preference (like so much cooking, come to think of it!). Blanching makes konjac a little less 'quick and simple' (the ethos of this book), but you are welcome to add more labor to your cooking if you wish!

For konjac rice, you can give it more of a rice-like texture by dry roasting it for 15 minutes or so, drying it out a bit, which again, is more work to do and so that's considered to be an optional step.

Shirataki noodles just need a great sauce to go with.

TVP

TVP, or Textured Vegetable Protein, is your handy ground beef substitute. Use it in lasagna, stuffed peppers, Bolognese sauce, or for other ground beef dishes like sloppy joes sandwiches, stir fry for lettuce wrap filling, and so on. It's sold dehydrated, and adding boiling water and covering rehydrates it (follow the instructions on the package). If your sauce or surrounding ingredients are amazing, the TVP will taste amazing and you will quickly forget that it's not ground beef.

Vegetable Broth

It's worth getting into your weekly routine making batches of vegetable broth, because it's very handy, especially when you make your own soups and seitan. You can of course throw any veggies you want into a pot of simmering water, or buy bouillon cubes, or buy readymade veggie broth. Because I'm lazy and always seeking efficiencies, I keep my weekly vegetable broth batch down to a few ingredients (besides the water, of course):

a dozen slices of ginger root
1 large onion (white or yellow, whatever looks best in the store that day)
a dozen garlic cloves (peeled, of course)

Throw in some bay leaves if you are really aching to do that. When making the chowder, consider using a lot more vegetables than just these when making the stock, to get more flavor for that recipe.

I simmer this at medium low heat for ~30 minutes. You don't want to overcook as the vegetables might start converting to a bitter taste.

An advantage of this limited ingredient set is that I can directly use the cooked garlic and onions in a new batch of coconut rice (see the recipe in the Rice section). This simple stock helps me come up with new efficient ways to be lazy in my cooking, or at least save time when making coconut rice! If you plan to reuse the broth components in this way, make sure your ginger slices are very large so you can easily separate them from the garlic and onion pieces.

Salad Dressings and Marinades

Speaking of (extra virgin, typically) olive oil and vinegar, a collection of both in a range of in/fused varieties is one of the best shortcuts to instant world class flavors in your cooking, as already mentioned. Oil and vinegar mixes work great as salad dressings, marinades (e.g. for tofu and konjac slices) or as a nice glaze topping your veggie burgers.

If you're new to the oil and vinegar mix and match game, consider starting with these kinds of combinations:

Chipotle olive oil and chocolate dark balsamic vinegar
Green chili olive oil and mango white balsamic vinegar
Tuscan, Milanese Gremolata or Provençal herbed olive oil with orange white balsamic vinegar
Garlic olive oil and grapefruit white balsamic vinegar
Unflavored olive oil and 'plain ol'' dark balsamic vinegar (a classic dipping sauce for bread)

Also, adding a little flavored vinegar is a great way to enhance any glass of plain water, as noted in the Simple Fancy Water recipe.

In my neck of North America, my local small store chain that sells these amazing concoctions is called Olive the Best. The main supplier, however, is in Italy and they sell to differently branded stores in various regions and countries, so find out where you can obtain these great flavored fluids. While retailers of course sell these online, nothing beats going into the store and doing your own taste tests, either of each separately or in various mixed combinations, since they usually offer as many free tastes in tiny sipping cups as you wish to try. Their psychology is correct—the more you taste, the more you will buy!

Premium extra virgin olive oils such as those sold in these specialty shops can be used in cooking at up to 410°F/210°C, so it's a bit of a myth that you can't use extra virgin olive oil for cooking. If you need to heat at an even higher temperature, this book's alternative is avocado oil.

My recipes either call for premixing an oil and vinegar together— for example, by whisking them in a mixing bowl first, as you might do for a salad dressing or marinade—or to apply them in separate phases, such as marinating tofu slices in oil first, then adding a vinegar gloss on top after cooking. Throwing each separately onto a salad and then tossing the salad usually doesn't work as well compared to mixing them together first.

When dipping bread into a mix, keeping them separate works fine as you can use the bread to mix them together. So, just keep these differences in mind—as to how to combine them—as you play with the recipes. Also note that oil and vinegar do not really mix together without an emulsifier (such as dijon mustard), and so they will remain somewhat separate, though mixing them still does still help with flavor combinations.

Recipe Organization

I have found that the usual concepts of breakfast, lunch, dinner and snacks more or less break down when following a low carb vegan diet. Instead, I have organized the recipes into time-of-day neutral meal categories. Needless to say, you won't be eating bacon and eggs for breakfast, and steak for dinner! Or ice cream for dessert, etc…unless you are seeking high carb high fat vegan animal product imitation foods in their place. Changing your conception of what to eat during the day opens you up to a lot of new possibilities, and so I have not referred to categories like 'breakfast, lunch and dinner' much in the book.

Meal Plan for Weight Loss

Need to lose some weight? We've all been there. Thinking that a vegan low carb diet might be the route to take? Well, ok, we've not all been there, but that just means you're in the dietary avant-garde when it comes to Self and Planet Care.

The Mike Ludo diet is GUARANTEED to work towards your weight loss goals. By using this word, 'guarantee,' no, I won't refund your money for buying the book.

Rather, if the meals don't help you achieve your weight loss goals, just message me the receipt from your purchase, and I will donate the amount of my royalty to a charitable environmental or wildlife organization. That's how certain I am that my low carb vegan diet will help you lose weight.

A good weight loss plan has some variety but not too much. The problem with introducing too many different kinds of food into your routine is that it creates a lot of opportunities for extra unwanted calories — particularly from carbs and fats — to enter into your diet, because it increases the amount of nutritional information you need to keep paying attention to.

The Mike Ludo diet is all about convenient yet healthy laziness, so keep it simple.

While certainly other combinations of my meals will help you achieve your weight loss goals, the ones below have been field tested and if I am wrong, oh well, worthy planet-saving charities will get some extra giving from me!

Coffee or tea? Sure.

If using a nondairy milk, choose an unsweetened very low carb brand.
If using a sweetener, choose a natural one like stevia or monk fruit.

Breakfast (choose one, alternate as needed)

TVP Zucchini Hash
Guacamole & Tomato Toast

Egg Scramble
Pickled Veggie Mandala with Protein Core (or without protein core)

<u>Lunch (choose one, alternate as needed)</u>
Creamy Green Smoothie (multiple glasses are fine)
Simple Fancy Salad #1 (with or without tofu or seitan topper)
Simple Fancy Salad #2 (with or without tofu or seitan topper)
Celtuce & Tofu Salad

<u>For Dinner, choose anything on my list, EXCEPT:</u>
Any dish using a lot of vegan meat and cheese substitutes
Any dish that uses a lot of coconut oil or melted margarine
Any dish that uses bread or (almond flour, chickpea flour, etc.) batter
Any dish that has fruit in it

<u>Snacks (1–2 per day)</u>
Unsalted nuts or seeds (not the dried fruit part, which is better for cheat meals)
Baked Tofu Slices & Soft Boiled Garlic Cloves
Guacamole & Tomato Toast
Watercress Soup
Cauliflower Soup
Seaweed Mushroom Soup
Leftovers from the Pickled Veggie Mandala with Protein Core (or without protein core)

<u>Cheat Meals (1–2 per week, NOT whole cheat days!)</u>
Eat anything you want, either from my list or elsewhere, including the vegan gelato factory.

That's it, super easy :) If you come across any issues with the meal prep, just leave a note in the article's comments and I'll respond there.

<u>Disclaimer</u>
Remember to consult with your doctor before going on the Mike Ludo diet, so that they'll say something like, "Who? Never heard of

this guy. Oh no, another diet fad craze," etc. and then proceed to listen to whatever else they say.

Please be aware of any food allergies you may have since I certainly am not, and eat accordingly. Chew thoroughly, don't swallow too fast, eat while also drinking to lubricate your mouth and throat, and you should be fine.

Make sure your meal prep and cheat meals get you the iodine, B12 and other tricky nutrients you need to pay attention to when going on a vegan diet. Check your blood work regularly and I also recommend taking a multivitamin in case any nutrients fall through the cracks of your routine.

Did I mention consulting with your doctor, to place all legal responsibility on them rather than me?

Happy eating!

Ketosis and Caloric Deficit

Ketosis is a metabolic state where your body switches to another energy pathway, getting energy from ketones from the breakdown of fats instead of glucose derived from carbohydrates. Getting into a state of ketosis requires eating very few carbs per day, often expressed in guidelines as no more than 20 grams of net carbs but that will of course vary by your body size and your metabolism etc. You can check to see if you're in ketosis via over the counter tests such as strips that measure ketones in your urine or through blood or breath tests.

Caloric deficit simply means that in a given day, you've burned more calories than you've consumed, which will also force the body to burn fat. A low carb diet supports both strategies for weight loss. If your goal is ketosis, minimize those ingredients in recipes that have more carbs or eat smaller portions for meals (for instance. eat 2 instead of three slices of low carb toast for breakfast). If you fail to get into a measurable state of ketosis, you can still lose weight via calorie deficit.

This book's philosophy is that constantly measuring everything isn't very practical for everyday low carb vegan eating, so ultimately it's a matter of crafting meal plans that let you easily achieve your goals with minimal hassle. The recipes that follow which are a bit higher in carbs are clearly labeled as being more appropriate for cheat meals or weight maintenance rather than daily consumption with weight loss in mind. Those ingredients that are potentially higher in carbs and fat are also indicated so you can tweak the amounts you add to your versions of the dish (such as the aforementioned vegan ground chorizo, using it for flavor for weight loss goals versus getting more meaty satisfaction from it if your goals are weight maintenance).

Future Fusion

I think of these recipes as representing a Future Fusion cuisine, whereby 'future' has two meanings: the future of the planet's ecosystems—secured through more sustainable agricultural practices—and the future of our own lives and bodies, fostered by eating for longevity and health. Inspirations are taken from many international culinary traditions, and indeed it is highly likely that in any given day or even in a single meal, multiple cultural influences will be experienced.

The intention of this kind of global recipe design is not so much about trying hard to imitate popular cuisines or even to attempt cultural appropriation. Rather, establishing strong continuity with pre-existing dietary traditions, habits and our general likes when it comes to food is considered a strategic and effective way of making this kind of dietary practice, and the resulting health benefits, long lasting and permanently established in the routines of our lives.

Temperature

Heat on a stovetop is rather analog, as the terms High, Medium and Low are extremely vague and relative to what your machine outputs. The stove I use has High Simmer and Low Simmer settings beneath Low, and of course, there is plenty of dial room in between. My temperature indications should be taken as broad categories which you will have to finesse based on the cooking possibilities of your stovetop.

Origins of this Book

Do a YouTube search on "Pixelphonics - Interview with Michael Filimowicz" (my legal name, Mike Ludo being a pen name :) and you'll see me during my attendance at the Future Technologies academic conference talking on camera while weighing 350 pounds. You wouldn't know from this video clips that at the time, I was regularly lifting weights, doing hot yoga, running on my elliptical machine at home, going on long hikes in the Vancouver area mountains, eating whole (unprocessed) foods, and in general, doing quite a lot of things that one is 'supposed to do' to be healthy!

And yet clearly, I was not healthy. This was probably the busiest time of my professional life: I was teaching full time, working overtime as an administrator in dual roles (associate dean and program director at my university), and enrolled in a PhD program, courtesy of the tuition waiver job perk. I thought I was being very clever in my diet, for example by going to a specialty meat store to get locally sourced organic wild game meats, eating plenty of fruits and whole grain breads, and eating eggs from free running chickens. I ate plenty of fish, which is a great dietary source of daily industrial heavy metals. And of course, my ratio of white to red meat consumption was almost saintly, or at least what all the corporate marketing said it should be. I blamed my busy schedule and genes (both my parents were obese) for my body weight.

A blood test checkup revealed that I was becoming prediabetic. Both an uncle and a grandmother were also diabetic, so I went immediately onto a low carb diet that was very similar to the South Beach Phase 1 plan that I had had some success with a decade earlier. After about a year on my new routine, I lost 70 pounds and had reversed most of what was starting to become troubling in my blood work (fatty liver, blood sugar etc.), but my cholesterol hadn't improved much. My father had several heart attacks, and a grandfather died of sudden cardiac arrest while mowing the lawn one day, so I have always been concerned about my cardiovascular health, for instance by doing stress tests on treadmills in hospitals every few years, just to make sure that all was more or less ok, at least according to the electrodes!

As an experiment, I cut my egg consumption in half, for instance by eating one instead of two eggs every time I included them in a meal. After a year, my cholesterol levels had much improved (no red flags!), but I still saw plenty of room for improvement. This is when I decided to go completely vegan in my diet, since clearly animal products were still causing potential issues with my health, despite now being at a much more normal body weight.

I had been vegan and vegetarian during some of my years in grad school in the 1990s (my Masters, not the PhD), but I gained a lot of weight on those diets, because of the high carb content form beans, rice, pasta, bread, and potatoes, so I gave up on plant-based diets because I gained too much weight on them. I went back to a diet that included meat and dairy, in order to lose weight, actually!

There was a time in my youth, from around 14 to 19 years old, when I was very slim—I still remember my waist size for jeans was 32" — a result of running 5 miles a day. In high school, that was relatively easy to do, since there was a rectangular park near my home, Francis Park in South St. Louis, Missouri, that was a mile and a quarter around—do four laps of that, and that's five miles. Eventually, though, one has to move out of the house, go to university and that's where one discovers dorm life, all-you-can-eat buffets on the university meal plan, student friends who save money when going out by sharing pitchers of beer and large pizzas, and, well, so much for running five miles a day!

I had also moved north, first to Des Moines and then to Chicago, where the winters were colder and longer, which, from the standpoint of my fitness routine at the time, meant that the sidewalks I would normally jog on were covered in slippery ice for long stretches of the year. Not to mention the homework, and that my knees seemed to have sustained some minor injuries from all that daily running, which had produced as a nice side effect not just next-day endorphin highs, but allowed me to eat *whatever I want, whenever I want, as much as I want*—which the diet in this book also aims for, simply by changing the parameters of what I allow myself to choose from.

This relationship between running everyday and being slim instilled a false sense in me that body weight is proportional to the amount of exercise one does—just run more, bike more, and the pounds will come off! Well, maybe if running 5 miles a day, or cycling across the country and doing 50 miles a day, but other than extreme routines like that, like most people, I have found that hitting the bikes and treadmills and trails had very little effect on my body's fat stores. There is an intuition we have, that in order to achieve something, we have to do something, and so we think: to lose weight (doing something #!), I have to go to the gym (doing something #2).

In reality, we can also do something by *not* doing something. I actually learned this in my early 20s reading zen philosophy, the idea of No Mind, or hitting the target (the zen of archery) without actually aiming for it. We can lose weight simply by not doing something, which in the context of this book, means to just stop consuming certain kinds of foods. Lots of body weight can be shed through non-action, so instead of hitting the streets and gyms and trails—the illusion that we need to work very hard to lose weight—if we just stop eating so many carbs (and unhealthy fats), the weight will just come off and it will seem like we lost weight by doing nothing at all!

I have also experienced unexpected health benefits from a low carb diet, such as the total disappearance of gastroesophageal reflux disease (GERD) which I developed as an undergrad during those long hours studying in the coffee shops. For decades, I was popping antacids—some over the counter, some prescribed—and was always told by my doctors to lay off the coffee, tomatoes and citrus. None of those MDs told me to lay off the carbs! But voilà, just cutting out the bread, potatoes, rice and pasta made my heartburn go away, and no amount of coffee drinking or tomato eating has brought it back. It's often the case that you can't trust the doctors too much, because their training is so narrowly specialized. General practitioners aren't trained well in nutrition, and nutritionists aren't trained well in medicine.

Additionally, you have the collusion between Big Pharma—producing all the drugs to treat lifestyle diseases—the Corporate Food Giants, who lobby the politicians to protect their junk food industries—and a political system that sends politicians into the arms of Big Pharma and the Corporate Food Giants in search of campaign funds. Thus, modern societies' health outcomes are a disaster, and it doesn't help that medicine and nutrition are siloed professionally, or that doctors are paid to dispense lifestyle disease treating drugs to their patients as a marketing practice. Ultimately, 'we the people' have to take things into our own hands as much as possible, especially when it comes to diet, because hell if governments or involved professional organizations will help us much.

So I have returned to a purely plant-based diet in my early 50s, having learned my nutritional lessons 'the hard way' as they say, understanding some of the pitfalls of vegan and vegetarian diets—how their high carb count can thwart one's health and body weight goals—and the limitations of all the so-called 'healthy' choices when it comes to consuming animal products. There is plenty of research that suggests the body has rather impressive capabilities of healing itself if only given a decent chance, and the longer I am on the low carb vegan diet described in this book, the more I continue to see improvements on a range of health markers.

In this book I am sharing what works for me, and of course everyone's body is different. There are no claims to anything scientific or authoritative in the recipes that follow. This project is entirely based on understanding my own experiences with food and shaping a routine that works for me. But I am also sure that it will work for many others as well, since while nutrition can be confusing due to all the contradictory information that keeps hitting our news feeds—where what was bad for you yesterday is healthy for you today and will become bad for you again tomorrow—I don't delve deeply into the latest and trendiest research, and instead stick to general practical principles that anyone can grasp and apply. And so, in the following pages, I have aimed for a well-rounded collection of easy to follow recipes that serve the purposes of everyday eating on a low carb vegan diet.

The Recipes

<u>Smoothies</u>

The Creamy Green Smoothie

The Creamy Green Smoothie is something I recommend drinking daily (or almost every day) since it's a 'super super' food because it combines many foods in themselves considered to be super foods! One batch of this smoothie makes 5 large glasses (in my blender at least), which I usually spread out over two days, though I have been known to drink all 5 in one day!

I use a large (2.5 liter) heavy duty blender for this, because it has to handle a lot of ingredients:

1 liter of unsweetened plain or vanilla almond milk (or use soy if you prefer)
2 tbsp apple cider vinegar
2 scoops of vegan protein powder supplement
2 tbsp of flaxseed oil
½ cup of ground flax seed, chia seed and hemp hearts blend
2 tsp of (fine powdered) psyllium husks
1 heaping tsp of matcha powder
1 heaping tsp of the Super Spice blend (see the Pantry Stocking section above)
1 ½ - 2 cups of sliced (thawed from frozen) avocado
3 tbsp of peanut or nut/seed butter
1 cup green tea
1 bag of frozen broccoli or kale (you can place it in frozen directly)

Variation: use fresh greens instead of previously frozen, such as half a box of baby spinach, or fresh green mix, or kale.

Variation: you can also add powdered spirulina (algae), though it can be a bit messy as it gets sticky when wet.

Makes 5 servings.

Usually to make something creamy, you add cream! The creaminess of this smoothie comes from the combination of peanut (or other nut and seed) butter, avocado chunks and the flax oil (which is full of polyunsaturated fats). I used to make this smoothie with two liters of almond milk, but I decided that overdosing on calcium is probably not a great idea. So, the current recipe uses just one liter of almond milk (unsweetened, plain or vanilla) and makes up for the extra liquid needed with green tea and water.

Note that chia seeds, hemp hearts and flaxseed together provide the amino acids threonine and lysine, which are lacking in seitan, and so if you go with seitan as a major source of protein, you are picking up these missing amino acids in the smoothie instead. Remember, you don't have to combine all amino acids in a single meal to get a complete protein—your body can get the protein it needs if the amino acids are consumed in your daily diet as a whole.

In Asian supermarkets, it's usually easy to find large bottles of unsweetened green tea, so I stockpile these in the pantry, and in the smoothie I add a cup. Once all the ingredients are in, top off the rest of the blender with water, making sure to keep a couple inches free at the top, so it doesn't overspill or spurt out when blending. The amount of water you add at the end affects how creamy or watery or thick the resultant smoothie is. Over time, you will get the hang of it and eyeball the proportions correctly to get it creamy every time.

Creamy Fruit Smoothie

This smoothie is a celebration of the fruits that have the lowest amount of carbs per volume, compared to most sweet fruits— excluding avocados, olives and tomatoes, of course--namely raspberries, blackberries, and strawberries.

Simply swap out the main green ingredient of the Creamy Green Smoothie—the kale, spinach, mixed greens etc.--and replace it with one of the low carb fruits (or a mix of them) mentioned above. This smoothie should be reserved for cheat meals for those with weight loss goals.

Body Smoothy

No, the name of the recipe is not a typo, since this smoothie makes the body smoothy.

Handling a huge fun-to-squeeze leaf of aloe vera makes me dream of being an herbivorous dinosaur nibbling on this plant 70 million years ago. Is that weird? It's just so smooth and spiky, and it feels like the kind of ergonomic gel pad you might use when typing at your keyboard, which, now that I think of it, is probably another great use for this leaf!

Aloe vera gel contains vitamins A, C, and E, which are popular in expensive skin creams — usually the more of these vitamins are packed into a cream or lotion, the more it costs. Each letter of the vitamin alphabet is like another *kaching, kaching* at the cash register. The aloe vera leaf also contains polysaccharides, phytosterols, enzymes, minerals (zinc, copper, magnesium), anthraquinones, amino acids, gibberellins and auxins. A leaf of aloe vera is like a molecular Who's Who? of compounds you read about on skin cream labels, ads and online descriptions. Its pH balance is also suitable for direct application to skin and hair.

One aloe vera gel leaf, though, costs just ~$2 Canadian dollars in my area, versus 10–50 times that to get creams that contain similar ingredients on the shelves at Sephora. In this time of runaway global inflation and stagnant wages, you might think that making your own skin cream with a two dollar leaf would be something everyone is doing at home.

Caveat: everyone's skin is different and who knows, yours may not take to an application of raw aloe vera gel, so rub a little bit on a patch of your skin before using it all over your body and hair, just to make sure your epidermis is accepting of it. If your skin starts to itch, puff up, boil, blister, or little gremlin versions of you start popping out of your hide and run crazy around the place, that's probably a good idea not to use it as a skin cream or in hair care. You can also try diluting it with water, if you find it's a tad strong for your skin.

Making aloe vera gel cream is easy but there are a few steps. First, cut off the ends and spiky edges, so you can see the gel-stuff all the way around the leaf.

You now need to soak it for around 30 minutes because in addition to the whitish stuff you see (the aloe vera gel), there's also a yellowish brown substance that is latex (also called aloe latex), which has laxative properties. Relieving constipation has been one of its uses in traditional remedies.

That being said, the FDA does not approve ingesting aloe vera gel and so I won't recommend it, but online there are plenty of videos of people eating aloe vera gel and not dying, for what it's worth. Soaking the trimmed aloe leaf in a large bowl for at least half an hour helps flush out the laxative latex substance, and this article is mainly interested in the white substance for topical (not internal consumption) uses.

Aloe gel is quite slimy, and I don't find that there's a high need for slimy food in my diet, since okra presents enough of a slime-challenge. I used to eat escargot but my days of eating slimy animals are over. Can you think of any food where sliminess would really bring out the flavor notes or provide a needed contrast in texture? Online videos show people blending aloe gel into smoothies — to make them slimier — or just licking the gel out of the leaf directly, which is kinda sexy.

After soaking it for at least half an hour, make a small notch with a sharp knife to separate the green leaf away from the gel at one side of the larger end, just enough to give you some fingertip room. And with that fingertip room, peel that side of the leaf away from the gel just using your hand, with the leaf end pinched in your fingers.

With the knife, scrape the white gel off the other leaf face, and any remaining on the leaf face you started with (you're basically fileting it). Scrape it off onto a large baking sheet or bowl or whatever makes sense to you as a place to scrape slimy gel onto. Once you're done scraping, just put it into a small food processor or blender and hit the atomize button.

You can pour the liquified gel through a large tea strainer to remove any larger chunks that didn't get processed, leaving you with a very nice gel cream.

Since it is fresh food, it will go bad, as there are no expensive cosmetic ingredients in there putting it into suspended animation for a long shelf life, so store it in your fridge and use it on your skin and hair for a similar number of days that you'd be willing to eat anything refrigerated after it's been cooked or prepped.

Keeping it in the fridge is also handy if you use alcohol-based hand sanitizers in the home. Since I have a dog, I am frequently handling raw meat and need to clean my hands well afterwards with everyone's favorite post-Covid molecule. After applying the hand sanitizer, I follow up with the aloe gel to restore my hands and wrist. You can also freeze it if you think you may not use all the gel before its freshness expires.

This homemade two dollar gel also works as a great after shave, and I should know, since I shave my head. My face and head composite makes for one large shaving surface area, and why pay Nivea for Vitamin E infused shaving balm when I can just go to my fridge and rub chilled aloe gel all over my head for pennies on the dollar?

Toasts & Paninis

Paninis

'Panini' is the Italian word for 'patience.' Ok, that's not true, but in spirit it is. A good panini is all about taking it slow. If you've ever found yourself at a café growing impatient because the panini is taking so long to make, you will understand why once you start making them yourself at home. Of course, you will need a panini maker! And sliced low carb bread.

Since it takes so long to grill a panini, you may as well take your time preparing it. Panini-ing is slow grilling, where you wrap a sandwich in wax or parchment paper, making sure that the outer edges of the sandwich are brushed with oil or vegan margarine so that you get the nice dark parallel stripes across the outer sides, which is like proof to the world that it is a panini.

So, take your time making it. With a panini, every little bit of attention and care you take will have big payoffs. A few pieces of fresh herbs here and there, a thin layer of pesto spread across one edge, getting the thickness of a tomato slice just right, deciding whether a tapenade should go at the bottom or top of the layers—these micro decisions will make a huge difference in the whole experience of eating it.

Then, there's the wait time. Make sure to preheat the panini while you are preparing it—you may as well, in the interest of time efficiency, so the slow grilling can start immediately once you place your paper-wrapped sandwich into the electric maw. Somewhere between 8-15 minutes of slow grilling works well, depending on how warm, smashed, dark lined, cheese melted, and flavor married you want the sandwich to be.

But wait, there's more slow to come! Because your panini will be very hot when it is done, too hot to eat, actually (without causing mouth injuries), you need to continue having patience and wait until it cools so you can finally enjoy it.

So, 'panini' really does mean 'patience' in Italian! Take your time making the sandwich, slow grilling it, and cooling it down. Making paninis is worthy of a Zen mindfulness ritual, analogous to the tea ceremony of Japan. Panini-zen certainly seems culturally needed in Italy, where it seems that, out on the streets, everyone is always trying to run you over in their honking speed-modified Vespas and amusingly tiny cars. Italy could really use a Panini Zen movement, if only to make it easier to cross the streets in one piece!

Seitanic Panini

If in Rome, I would advise against eating a Seitanic Panini if you happen to be within earshot of the Vatican, otherwise you are probably safe from tempting fate with this recipe. Seitan is the star of this meal, but not to worry—you can still get into vegan heaven by enjoying this meaty sandwich.

Use as much chopped up precooked seitan as you can reasonably expect to fit onto a single sandwich, perhaps ~½ cup depending on how good your sandwich holding skills are—see the Seitan recipe in the Protein section.

2 slices of low carb bread
1-2 tbsp garlic flavored extra virgin olive oil (the garlic helps keep the undead away)
1 tbsp burning hot sauce (go as high up the Scoville scale as you dare)
1 tsp truffle sauce
2 tbsp sun-dried tomatoes
1-2 tbsp ajvar
Fresh herbs: oregano or basil, anyone?

Makes 1 serving.

Preheat the panini maker.

While it's warming up, brush all sides of the bread slices with the olive oil. Brush onto one of the inside slices layers of the hot sauce, truffle sauce, and ajvar. Add a layer of sun-dried tomatoes, then pile on a heaping spread out mound of the seitan.

You want the sandwich to be thick, but not have the seitan falling out constantly when you eat it. The seitan should be cut up into smallish pieces so you don't have to chew through a huge piece to take a bite of the sandwich. Add some fresh herbs that make you think of Italy. Now cover the layers with the remaining slice of bread.

Wrap the sandwich in wax paper or parchment paper, and grill inside the panini maker for ~10 minutes. Let cool before eating.

Greco Roman Panini

2 slices low carb bread
Herbal flavored extra virgin olive oil (Tuscan, Milanese Gremolata or Provençal)
Two tomato slices
Vegan feta cheese block
Vegan pepperoni roll
Fresh herbs: thyme and oregano

Makes 1 serving.

Preheat the panini maker.

While it's warming up, brush all sides of the bread slices with the olive oil. With a mandolin, cut slices of tomato, vegan pepperoni roll and vegan feta cheese. On the inside of the sandwich, neatly arrange these slices and add fresh herbs (the herbs are what really make this a Next Level low carb vegan panini).

Wrap the sandwich in wax paper or parchment paper, and grill inside the panini maker for ~10 minutes.

Keep in mind that vegan cheese has non-trivial amounts of fat and sometimes carbs (as may the pepperoni roll), so read the label and adjust portion sizes to your goals (weight loss, cheat day, general practical veganism, etc.). In the photos, this sure looks a lot like the grilled cheese described below! The differences, of course, are the feta, and the cool panini stripes.

Seoulfood Punini

Sorry for the bad joke in this recipe's name, but it's always good to keep the humor cogs greased up no matter what kind of bad dad joke might come out.

4 slices of low carb bread (for 2 sandwiches)
1–2 tbsp garlic flavored extra virgin olive oil (or any oil except motor oil)
½ cup finely scissored vegan kimchi (1/4 cup per sandwich)
6 slices (3 per sandwich) of baked marinated tofu

Makes 2 servings.

Preheat the panini maker.

While it's warming up, brush the outer faces of the bread slices with the olive oil.

Add the kimchi and baked tofu slices (usually 3 slices from a block of marinated baked tofu works) and close the sandwich.

Wrap the two sandwiches in wax paper or parchment paper, and grill inside the panini maker for ~15 minutes. Let cool before eating.

Breakfast Panini

4 slices of low carb bread (for 2 sandwiches)
1–2 tbsp garlic flavored extra virgin olive oil (or any oil except motor oil)
1 cup prepared egg scramble (~½ cup per sandwich, see the recipe in the Protein + Veggies section)
Fresh basil or oregano (optional)

Makes 2 servings.

Preheat the panini maker.

While it's warming up, brush the outer faces of the bread slices with the olive oil.

You want the sandwich to be thick, but not have the egg scramble falling out constantly when you eat it. Once it has been panini'd, the scramble will behave very well inside the boundaries of the toast, due to food physics. Spread the egg scramble on the inner face of each sandwich-to-be.

Add some fresh herbs that make you think of Italy if you like, on top of the scramble layer. Now cover with the remaining slice of bread, making sure you are keeping the oiled sides on the outside faces of the sandwich, since that gives you very nice parallel grill stripes on the toast.

Wrap the two sandwiches in wax paper or parchment paper, and grill inside the panini maker for ~12 minutes. Let cool before eating.

Whole Fruit and Nut/Seed Butter Toast

1-3 slices of low carb whole wheat bread, toasted
2 tsp-1 tbsp of nut/seed butter (of your choice) per slice
2 tbsp- ½ cup thawed frozen blackberries, raspberries or
strawberries per slice
Variation #1: ½ cup baked apple slices per slice (see the recipe for
the baked apples in the dessert section)

Variation #2: sprinkle leftover toasted coconut flakes from the
Coconut Rice recipe (in the Rice section) on the nut or seed butter,
either by itself or as a layer under the fruit.

Makes 1 serving.

This is my low carb take on the peanut butter and jelly classic.
Remember, nut and seed butters on whole grain low carb toast
make a complete protein.

 Fruit is full of sugar, so jams, jellies and compotes are somewhat
overkill, or at least highly redundant, in adding sugar to food that
is already loaded with sugar. Just toast (in a toaster oven) some
low carb bread slices, spread on a nut/seed butter of your choice,
and on top of that, place whole fruit instead of jelly or jam. Eat
open face style.

The fruit will generally stick easily to the nut/seed butter, though
whole blackberries might roll off so handle gingerly. You can also
puree the fruit in a small food processor if you prefer a texture
that's more like jam and jelly so that it is more easily spreadable.
The baked apple variation has more carbs and so is better for
cheat meals or when your goals are weight maintenance.

Lentil Paté Mini Toast

3 slices of low carb bread
A roll of lentil paté (store bought)
Flavored extra virgin olive oil (herbal or garlic)
Fresh herb garnish (optional)

Makes 1 serving or several smaller snacky servings.

Cut the edge crusts off the three slices of the bread to make neat rectangular shapes of their soft centers. Reserve the crust, to be used later for either croutons—see the recipe for Simple Fancy Salad #2 in the Veggies section—or the Toasted Bread Crust Sticks in the Snacks section.

Cut each crustless rectangular bread piece in half, making six small slices total. Brush the flavored olive oil across all the bread slices. Toast (a toaster oven works best) to a nice golden brown color. Cut six slices from the lentil paté roll and place one slice on each piece of bread. As a variation, you can put the paté on the slices before they go into the toaster oven to make them warm and melty. Garnish with some fresh herbs on top, if desired.

Depending on the thickness of the lentil paté slices, this meal may be better for a cheat day or for weight maintenance rather than weight loss goals.

Hummus and Tomato Toast

1-3 slices of low carb bread, toasted
2 tsp-1 tbsp of hummus (of your choice) per slice
Slice(s) of tomato (depends on how large your tomato is) per slice
Fresh ground salt and pepper to taste

Variation #1: there are a wide range of hummus flavors easily available in stores, so consider variations with pine nuts (shown in the photo at medium.com/low-carb-vegan on the Toasts page) and other great flavors.

Variation #2: brush the top sides of the toast with flavored extra virgin olive oil.

Makes 1 serving.

Hummus, being legume based, has more carbs the more of it you eat, so spread very lightly if your goal is weight loss, and more generously if it's weight maintenance. Add a few slices of tomato on top along with fresh ground salt and pepper.

Guacamole and Tomato Toast

1-3 slices of low carb bread, toasted
1-3 tbsp of guacamole per slice
Slice(s) of tomato (depends on how large your tomato is) per slice
Fresh ground salt and pepper to taste

Variation: brush the top sides of the toast with flavored extra virgin olive oil.

Makes 1 serving.

Guacamole is a classic 'good fat' food, derived as it is from avocados. In blood tests, one of the key markers tracked is the ratio of good to bad cholesterol, or HDL to LDL, respectively. While the diet in this book is full of many foods that support good cholesterol levels (a plant-based diet in general is associated with lower overall cholesterol), the guacamole in this toast is an important source of healthy fats.

Marmite Toast

1-3 slices of low carb bread, toasted
1 tbsp of marmite per slice

Variation: add a layer of honey on cheat meals, to tame or at least contrast the salty umami flavor.

Makes 1 serving.

Marmite is one of those foods that makes you think, "Huh, someone had the idea to invent this." It is made from yeast extract which is a byproduct of beer making. The folks who invented it were thinking, it seems, "Hmmm, after making beer, what do we do with all this yeast extract stuff?" and then someone said, "Hey, let's spread it on toast!" or something like that.

Its flavor is strong in saltiness, umami and savory notes (I think of it as basically like a salty honey). It is fortified with various nutrients to make it more worth eating, including B vitamins, in particular B12, because these clever folks thought it should be marketed to vegans and vegetarians.

Bruschetta

3 slices low carb bread
2 tbsp garlic flavored extra virgin olive oil
toppings, such as: ajvar, vegan cheese, olive tapenade and dill
almond pesto

Makes 1 serving.

Trim the crusts off three slices of bread, and brush the slices with
the oil. Toast until nice and crisp. Then, add a different topping to
each one, so you have a nice colorful collection of low carb
bruschetta! Use the cheese as a base for any of the other
recommended toppings above. Reserve the bread crusts for use as
bread sticks (see the Snacks section) or as croutons (see Simple
Fancy Salad #2 in the Veggies section).

Pizza'd Grilled Cheese

2 slices of low carb bread
A block of vegan cheddar or gruyere cheese
Vegan pepperoni roll (store bought)
2 tbsp Vegan margarine spread

Makes 1 serving.

Preheat a skillet at low heat.

Repeatedly run the pepperoni roll end-wise across the smallest
sized setting of a mandolin, so that you get a mound of thin
circular vegan pepperoni pieces. From the cheese block, slice off a
thin piece from the top edge so that you get a square slice of
cheese.

Place two slices of the bread on top of each other. On the outer
edges of the sandwich, lather the margarine spread (I like the kind
derived from olive oil). Place the cheese slice inside along with as
many of the pepperoni slices as will reasonably fit.

Place the sandwich onto the hot skillet, sliding the sandwich around a little bit to make sure the bread is evenly coated with the margarine as it starts to melt, and then cover the skillet (covering it will increase the heat and help the cheese melt faster, since vegan cheese can be somewhat melt-resistant). Flip the sandwich over a few times, taking care not to burn it, and making sure you get appropriate browning of the bread.

Because of the fat content from the margarine and cheese, this meal is better for a cheat day or for weight maintenance rather than weight loss goals.

Pastas & Sauces

The pasta recipes rely on shirataki, which is the noodle form of konjac (Japanese name: konnyaku). Konjac is gelatinous and somewhat translucent, produced from the corm of a Southeast Asian tuber. Konjac is rich in a dietary fiber, glucomannan, which has very few calories. Konjac can be used as noodles, rice or blocks (to be cut up into strips or cubes), and produces a strong sense of fullness. It is actually mostly water, and acts well as a 'sponge' by taking in the flavors of surrounding ingredients.

Carbonara #1

Nope, "carbonara" is not Italian for "carb sauce," especially in this version.

1 package of shirataki (white noodles), 200g
2-3 strips (per serving) of vegan bacon
1 tsp extra virgin olive oil (for cooking the bacon)
1 cup ground almonds
½ cup nutritional yeast
2 tbsp extra virgin olive oil (for the sauce)
1 tbsp soy sauce or tamari
1 tsp dijon mustard
1 tsp garlic powder
½ tsp onion powder
Salt and pepper to taste

Variation: for more sauciness, add a splash of cashew milk after blending. For less sauciness, let the soaked ground almonds sit awhile, as the sauce will thicken over time.

The sauce makes 4-6 servings, while each package of shirataki noodles is one serving.

In a bowl, pour 1 cup of very hot water onto the ground almonds, stir and let soak for 1 hour.

One hour later, pour into the soaked ground almonds all the remaining ingredients (except for the shirataki noodles and bacon—and the 1 tsp of oil for heating the bacon, of course). Stir to thoroughly mix the ingredients, then pour everything into a blender to *really* mix it all together (this takes ~10 seconds).

Heat 1 tsp of olive oil in a small skillet. Scissors the bacon strips into very little pieces (imagine bacon confetti), and transfer the little vegan bacon bits into the skillet, where it shall be sizzled and cooked in ~2 minutes.

Strain the excess water from the shirataki package. Microwave the shirataki noodles by themselves, covered on high for 90 seconds, again straining any excess water from the noodles. Transfer the shirataki noodles to a mixing bowl, then pour ¼ cup or so of the sauce from the blender into the bowl (adjust amount for taste and sauciness). Sprinkle the cooked vegan bacon confetti onto the pasta, give it all another toss and you're good to go.

Optionally, sprinkle onto the carbonara grated vegan cheese and fresh ground pepper, if those flourishes rock your gondola.

Carbonara #2

This is an alternative version of shirataki carbonara. Both are great but taste very different, which makes the concept of doing shirataki pastas all the more intriguing.

1 package of shirataki (white konjac noodles), 200g
¼ cup Egg Yolk Substitute (see the recipe in the Protein section)
Garnish with parsley
Pepper (not salt!) to taste
Grated vegan cheese (optional, to taste)

Strain the excess water from the shirataki package. Microwave the shirataki noodles, covered on high for 90 seconds, again straining any excess water from the noodles.

Transfer the shirataki noodles to a mixing bowl, then pour ¼ cup of the egg yolk substitute and toss to coat the noodles with the sauce, adding pepper to taste (remember that the egg yolk substitute has plenty of black salt, so no more salt is needed). While tossing, you can add some grated vegan cheese if so desired.

Transfer to a bowl and garnish with the parsley.

Pesto Pasta

1 package of shirataki (white noodles), 200g
1 tsp garlic or herb flavored extra virgin olive oil
2 tbsp dill and almond pasta
1 tbsp grated vegan parmesan cheese (sprinkle to taste)

Makes 1 serving.

Strain excess water from the shirataki package. In a mixing bowl, combine the shirataki, olive oil, and pesto, mixing them gently with a fork. Microwave covered for 90 seconds on high, again straining any excess water. Sprinkle with the parmesan.

Variations: try other pestos! Read the label first and check for fat and carb content to stay within your dietary goals.

Creamy Alfredo Sauce

To get creamy low carb vegan anything, you usually need to start with silken tofu and a nondairy milk like cashew milk. That's your cream base, and while it's not exactly flavorless, you should think of it as a canvas on which to compose something that will please your palette.

Italian cuisine is very approachable in that it usually just consists of a relatively small number of easily identifiable (like, what you see is what you get) high quality ingredients, combined with a simplicity often verging on minimalism. Italian food is peasant and worker food elevated to world class cuisine (or so says Stan Tucci), and that 'keep it simple and natural' ethos is what you should keep in mind when doing Italian anything. It's also why I find Italy (not North American Italian restaurants!) so inspiring for food ideas.

To the silken tofu and nondairy milk base, good choices for additional ingredients would be onion powder, minced garlic or garlic powder of soft boiled garlic cloves, truffle sauce, smoked paprika, salt and pepper. To make it a bit more complex, you can add a tablespoon of herb-flavored extra virgin olive oil, a pinch of saffron and a dash of black salt (kala namak). Garnish with fresh parsley or basil.

That's all a cream sauce needs for flavor-punch, and using silken tofu will give you a proper amount of complete protein. This sauce works well for creamy pastas as well as a creamy base for flatbreads and pizzas.

1 package silken tofu, ~400g
½ cup nondairy milk, consider cashew milk
1 tsp Tuscan (or other) herb flavored extra virgin olive oil
1 tsp truffle sauce
1 tsp onion powder
1 tbsp nutritional yeast
5–8 soft boiled garlic cloves (see the recipe in the Veggies section)
Fresh ground pepper to taste
Fresh ground black salt (kala namak) to taste
Fresh parsley to garnish.

This sauce makes 4 servings for pasta or covers one phyllo dough pizza.

Put all of the above (except for the fresh herb garnish) into a food processor or blender, and creamify everything. Add more nondairy milk to thin the sauce if you want a less creamy cream sauce. Warm on the stove before serving if using on pasta.

Usually each bag of shirataki noodles makes for one serving of the pasta part.

For pizza ideas, see the Cream Sauce Pizza ideas in the next section.

Ground Beef Stroganoff

2 packages shirataki noodles, ~400g each (thick linguini style)
2 tbsp herb flavored extra virgin olive oil (Tuscan, Milanese
Gremolata or Provençal)
2 medium onions, finely chopped
10 big brown cremini mushrooms, coarsely chopped
2 cups rehydrated TVP
2 ½ cups Creamy Alfredo Sauce (see the previous recipe)
Salt and pepper to taste
1 cup fresh parsley
Truffle oil (optional garnish when serving)
1 tbsp nutritional yeast (optional garnish when serving)

Makes 6 servings.

In a large skillet, heat the oil at low medium heat and sauté the
onions and mushrooms until the vegetables are halfway soft. Add
the rehydrated TVP, and salt and pepper to taste. Pour in the
Creamy Alfredo Sauce and stir, bringing it all to a simmer. Add in
the shirataki noodles and parsley, stir again, cook covered for a
few more minutes to help the flavors marry or at least date.

When serving, you can top with a sprinkling of nutritional yeast or
truffle oil for extra impact.

Marinara Sauce

Keep a batch of this homemade tomato sauce handy in the fridge
for use in pastas, lasagnas and rice dishes. Tomatoes come in
various sizes, so the ingredients below provide a general guideline
since it's a good idea to experiment with different tomato
varieties.

10 roma (also called 'plum') tomatoes
1 tsp garlic powder
1 tsp onion powder
1 tsp dried oregano
1 tsp hot cayenne (if spiciness is desired)

1 tsp dried basil
1 tbsp minced garlic
1 tbsp stevia or monk fruit
1 tbsp herbal flavored extra virgin olive oil (Tuscan, Milanese Gremolata or Provençal)
Salt and pepper (to taste)
Fresh oregano and basil (add after cooking)
1 tbsp Guar gum or xanthan gum (optional, thicken to taste)

Cooking the sauce works well in a slow cooker that has a groove for a serving spoon between the pot and the lid—slow cookers that also work as party food warmers will have this. This opening allows water to evaporate, which is critical for evaporating the water to get a thicker sauce. If you can't thicken the sauce this way with a slow cooker, after cooking it, you can transfer to a large pot and simmer until enough water has evaporated, or optionally, use a thickener like guar gum or xanthan gum to finish the thickening job (but just a little, so it doesn't become puffy—no one likes puffy tomato sauce).

In a blender, liquify the roma tomatoes, and transfer to a slow cooker. Add the remaining ingredients (except for the fresh herbs), stir, and cook at the low setting for 8 hours, stirring occasionally and seasoning for taste (taste test while it's cooking). Thicken the sauce as discussed above, if needed. You can cook on high as well (it's very hard to overcook in a slow cooker) to speed up evaporation of the water, which thickens the sauce.

Add in the fresh basil and oregano before serving.

Marinara Pasta

1 package of shirataki (white noodles), 200g
1 cup of the Marinara Sauce (recipe above)
2 tbsp olive tapenade
1 tbsp small capers
1 tbsp grated vegan parmesan cheese (sprinkle to taste)
Fresh basil

Makes 1 serving.

Heat the marinara sauce in a saucepan. Strain excess water from the shirataki package. Microwave on high covered for 90 seconds, again straining any excess water. Transfer to a bowl. Spoon the marinara sauce on top of the shirataki. Add the tapenade, capers and fresh basil. Sprinkle with the parmesan and serve.

Bolognese Pasta

1 package of shirataki (white noodles), 200g
1 ½ cup of the Marinara Sauce (see the recipe above)
⅓ cup dry TVP (textured vegetable protein)
1-2 tbsp grated vegan parmesan cheese (optional)
Parsley to garnish (optional)

Variation: mix the rehydrated TVP with the Red Pepper Sauce (recipe below) instead of the Marinara Sauce.

Makes 1 serving.

Rehydrate the TVP following the instructions on the package.

Simmer the marinara sauce and add in the rehydrated TVP which is essentially your faux ground beef for the Bolognese sauce. Simmer for 5 minutes so the TVP really gets into a marinara mood, which will put you into a Bolognese mood.

Strain excess water from the shirataki package. Microwave the noodles on high, covered, for 90 seconds, again straining any excess water. Transfer to a bowl. Spoon the Bolognese sauce on top of the shirataki and perhaps sprinkle with grated vegan parmesan cheese if desired. Garnish with fresh parsley.

Chorizo Pasta

1 package of shirataki (white noodles), 200g
1 tsp garlic flavored extra virgin olive oil
2-4 tbsp vegan ground chorizo
½ -1 tbsp grated vegan parmesan cheese (sprinkle to taste)

Makes 1 serving.

Strain excess water from the shirataki package. In a mixing bowl, combine the shirataki, olive oil, and chorizo, mixing them gently with a fork. Microwave covered for 90 seconds on high, again straining any excess water. Sprinkle with the parmesan.

The ground vegan chorizo will have carbs and fat levels that can affect your goals of either weight loss or maintenance—as will the fat in the vegan cheese—so read the nutritional labels of those items and vary the amount you use accordingly (using it either for flavoring or to get more meatiness and cheesiness).

Red Pepper Sauce Pasta

1 package of shirataki (white noodles), 200g
2 tbsp garlic flavored extra virgin olive oil
1 small onion, chopped
1 tbsp minced garlic, with the water squeezed out
1 cup ajvar (red pepper spread, read the labels for the lowest carb content brand)
1 can (14 oz) unsweetened diced tomatoes, not strained.
1 tsp dried oregano
1 tsp dried basil
Salt and pepper to taste
Crushed red pepper flakes to taste (optional)
Fresh parsley (for garnish)

The sauce makes 4 servings.

Variation: Shirataki also comes in a brown color, in case you get bored of seeing white noodles all the time. The brown kind also releases less water when microwaved.

Don't forget to wear swimming goggles when chopping the onion, so your eyes don't burn. Ski goggles also work, if you don't have the swimming kind.

In a saucepan, heat the olive oil over medium low heat. Add the onion first so it starts to soften, then add the garlic. Sauté until the onion is translucent and the garlic makes the area around the stove smell like garlic.

Stir in the ajvar (red pepper spread) and mix well with the onion and garlic, then add the diced tomatoes and stir again.

Add the oregano, basil, salt and pepper to taste. For extra heat, add the crushed red pepper to taste but also consider the taste of others you might feed this to, with respect to their Scoville scale tolerance. A little bit goes a long way, and a 'strong hint' of crushed chilis is all that's needed. You can complexify that strong hint by using a chili-flavored olive oil instead, which will make people go, "Huh, what's that chili combo?"

Bring to a simmer, then reduce heat and simmer for another ~10-15 minutes for flavor marrying and sauce thickening. Add water if needed to thin the sauce to a desired consistency.

While simmering, microwave (or otherwise heat) the shirataki noodles at high covered for 90 seconds.

Pour the sauce on a bowl of shirataki noodles (or zucchini noodle alternative, described below) and top with the fresh parsley. With the red pepper and parsley flavors, you totally do not need to sprinkle vegan grated parmesan cheese onto it.

Zucchini Pasta Variation

If you tire of konjac pasta, or even never got to like it in the first place, try zucchini pasta instead. Just like konjac, it will need to be strained when microwaved :) With the shredder insert on a mandolin (you can choose thicker or thinner shreds to your liking), run a zucchini lengthwise across the blades (watch your fingers!). You can also use a spiraling tool to achieve a similar end state. The longer the zucchini, the longer your green 'noodles' will be. You can boil or microwave the zucchini noodles to get them soft, and they will make for a nice alternative to konjac noodles.

Spinach Lasagna

1 ½ amazingly massive supremely large giant green zucchinis (or equivalent in smaller ones)
2 500g bags of thawed frozen spinach (or 4 250g bags, or 1 1kg bag, etc.)
2 454g packages of medium tofu (how and why they get to exactly 454g, I have no idea)
3 tbsp minced garlic
1 tbsp dried oregano
1 tbsp dried basil
2 cups sautéed onions or 2 tbsp onion powder
2 cups shredded vegan cheese, optional
4 cups marinara sauce (see the recipe above)
Salt and pepper, herbs and paprika to taste
1 tbsp avocado oil

Preheat the oven to 375°F. To get the celsius, $(375°F - 32) \times 5/9 =$???

With a mandolin at the thinnest setting, cut the washed zucchini lengthwise to make enough rectangular-ish slices that will make 3 layers of the lasagna in your casserole dish. Use scissors to cut a length to make the layers just the right size.

Place the thawed previously frozen spinach into a large colander, and press hard to squeeze the water out. It's a good idea to also let the spinach get room temperature, because at fridge temperature, wow your hands will be freezing after pressing the water out. As a good vegan, you might be tempted to drink the resultant pressed spinach water, but I'm not. Move the compacted spinach to a very large mixing bowl.

Drain the water from the 2 tofu packages and add the tofu to the mixing bowl with the spinach, then smash it all up, stirring and swirling them together. The key thing here is to trick the mind into believing visually that the tofu looks just like ricotta cheese, because spinach and ricotta is an actual culinary thing, and like ricotta, the tofu is white and full of protein. So, try to mix these two ingredients up as much as possible until you believe it looks like spinach and ricotta. Add in the minced garlic and dried spices while producing this optical illusion.

Add the vegan cheese if you like, just noting that the extra fat may thwart weight loss goals. The cheese will, of course, make this seem more like 'real' lasagna.

For the onion flavor, you can sauté white or yellow ones in oil and herbs (not all the way done, since they have to cook more in the oven with the lasagna) or just use a few tbsp of onion powder.

Salt, pepper, herbs and paprika to taste.

Coat a large deep casserole dish (the kind that seems very serious for a proper lasagna) with the avocado oil for non-stick purposes. Lay the first layer of zucchini, brush it with some marinara sauce, then apply half of the spinach-tofu mixture. Cover with a second layer of zucchini slices, brush with some more marinara sauce, and apply the remaining spinach-tofu mixture. Apply the final layer of zucchini slices, and brush with a more generous amount of marinara sauce.

Cover with foil and bake for 1 hour and 15 Imperial-Metric minutes. Then, remove the foil and bake for another 30 minutes so the tomato sauce on top caramelizes and more water in the filling can evaporate. Take a photo of your creation for social media with the text caption, "Huh, it looks like a vegan lasagna!"

Classic Lasagna

Follow the same steps as described above with the Spinach Lasagna, but switch out the spinach and tofu filling with the TVP mixture of the Stuffed Peppers recipe in the Protein + Veggies section.

Pizza

A box of thawed phyllo dough
A container of vegan margarine
Flavored extra virgin olive oil (for some variations)

Given the amount of vegan margarine and/or oil to make a good phyllo pizza crust, not to mention any vegan cheese you place on top, this style of pizza is probably better for cheat meals, or for weight maintenance rather than loss goals. I would be very surprised if you lost weight on a diet consisting entirely of phyllo dough pizzas, but at the same time, I would also be very delighted for you!

On the one hand, phyllo dough is extremely thin and almost gossamer when you handle it (every book should use the word 'gossamer' at least once!). On the other hand, it is very forgiving, and if you end up with some torn sheets or crumpled edges, just straighten it up as best you can because the phyllo layers working together are not designed to be pure Platonic geometric forms, architecturally speaking, and it really doesn't have to be pretty.

Warm some vegan margarine in a small pot on low heat, with the goal of melting it (or with the goal to stare at it melting, if that interests you). Line a large baking sheet—which should be large enough to easily place the phyllo dough on—with parchment paper. Place the first layer of phyllo dough on the parchment paper, and with a silicon brush, brush the melted margarine lightly across the surface. Don't worry about properly covering every exact square inch of the dough sheet, just kind spread it around in a thin layer with the brush. You can also mix extra virgin olive oil into the melted margarine because liquid fat is liquid fat.

If you've ever seen photographs or videos of Jackson Pollock painting large scale canvases by hurling paint at it from above, that's a bit like brushing margarine, oil, sauce and anything else onto phyllo dough. Treat it as your canvas, and be very pleased with the random patterns you make.

Now repeat—time for the second layer of phyllo dough. Just place it on top of the first layer, brush it with the melted margarine, and repeat. Repeat these steps until you have a base layer of 5-6 phyllo dough sheets, which is enough layers that will let you easily drag the pizza off the baking sheet and onto a cutting board, and from there, pick up each slice to eat handheld style. To achieve this soft yet crispy hand-holdable consistency, bake for 15 minutes at 375°F/190°C.

There are two recipes for phyllo dough pizza below, which present two different concepts illustrating what's possible in terms of the toppings you pile onto the phyllo crust. Following these, there's a whole section just on suggested topping combinations from a range of global cuisine influences. You can see photos of the phyllo dough pizzas at medium.com/low-carb-vegan on the Pizzas page.

Pepperoni

Marinara sauce (see the recipe in the Pastas section)
Vegan pepperoni log
Vegan shredded cheese package

Makes 6 servings.

Preheat the oven to 375°F/190°C.

Use a mandolin at the thinnest setting to cut many circular pieces off a vegan pepperoni log. Using your phyllo dough dexterity brushing skills, brush the marinara sauce on the top layer of phyllo dough. Distribute a layer of shredded cheese on top of the sauce, and on top of the cheese, distribute sliced rounds of the pepperoni. Bake for 15 minutes or until you approve of the phyllo goldenness.

Garlic or herb flavored extra virgin olive oil
Marinara sauce (see the recipe in the Pastas section)
A dozen pre-softened garlic cloves (boiled, baked or microwaved)
Capers (the small kind)
Olive tapenade
Fresh basil
Salad greens

Makes 6 servings.

Preheat the oven to 375°F/190°C.

The cooking time for this pizza is a lot less than what's needed to soften whole garlic cloves, so pre-soften them by boiling, baking or microwaving them. Or, use garlic cloves that have been softened up previously by flavoring a vegetable broth (that's my usual method).

The flavored olive oil in this recipe is for mixing with the melted margarine in the layers of phyllo. For example, a garlic flavored oil will reinforce the garlic cloves on the topping, whereas an herb flavored oil will reinforce the fresh herbs on top, so it's up to you!

Brush the marinara sauce on the top layer of phyllo dough, then evenly distribute the ingredients for the topping (but do not cover every square inch of the top layer—leave plenty of negative space where there's just some brushed marinara on the phyllo visible).

Bake for 15 minutes or until you approve of the phyllo goldenness.

Preheat the oven to 375°F/190°C.

Phyllo Dough Pizza Crust— Cooking Spray Method

With this variation, you are proceeding as usual with layering phyllo dough into 5-6 layers, as with the phyllo pizzas, pizza roll, burek, or fruit pizza—only, instead of melted margarine and/or oil, use cooking oil spray instead. Read the spray bottles carefully or do online research into the healthiest options, but in essence you want as few (if any) additives as possible so you are getting the oil in a light mist format.

Using cooking oil spray greatly lowers the calorie and fat content compared to brushed oil and melted margarine, though of course the experience and taste is less rich. You can still hand hold pizza slices, but they do not fold as well and may snap if you intend to fold a slice into a U-shape, so either do not fold it, take the risk of folding it, or just cut smaller slices that don't need to be folded. After refrigerating, the crust folds remarkably well, however, due to food physics, as moisture has been gradually absorbed into the crust as a function of time.

Recipe

Cooking spray (look for a very healthy choice, free of added chemicals, etc.)
6 layers of phyllo dough

In this much lower fat variation, instead of using melted vegan margarine and/or oil to brush on the phyllo layers, you are just using cooking oil spray, which usually has pretty much no nutritional value, according to the labels, other than not being loaded with fat.

So, just proceed the same otherwise—layer a baking sheet large enough for the phyllo dough layers with parchment paper. Lay the first phyllo layer, spray with cooking spray, lay the next phyllo layer, spray again, etc. until you have a raw crust of 5-6 layers.

Pizza Roll

The origins of this recipe are in undergrad dorm life, where I learned that my leftover pizza in the little fridge between the beds would usually get eaten by others before I could finish it. To thwart others from stealing my leftover pizza slices, I started ordering toppings I knew no one else would eat, so basically from a certain point forward every pizza I bough included green peppers, black olives and anchovies. Problem solved! No more stealing Mike's cold pizza slices.

This pizza roll is very artsy, because it makes you feel like a graffiti artist with spray paint in hand when applying the cooking spray to the phyllo dough, then you get to be a painter when you brush the filling on the top layer before rolling it. Get your avant-garde vibe on with this dish ;)

An uncooked phyllo dough pizza crust layered using the Cooking Spray method
2 tbsp avocado or extra virgin olive oil
1 cup shredded vegan cheese
1 cup dehydrated TVP
1 cup of the Marinara Sauce (see the recipe in the Pasta section)
Half a medium-sized onion, again cut in half for easier processing
6-8 garlic cloves
1 pasilla pepper, stem top cut off and deseeded then halved
1 tbsp Super Spice (see the recipe in the Pantry Stocking section)
2 cups coarsely chopped brown cremini mushrooms
Half can of pitted black olives (use ~200g or 7 oz)
3 heaping tbsp sun-dried tomatoes
2 tbsp black truffle sauce
Salt and pepper (to taste)

Rehydrate the TVP.

Heat the oil in a very large deep saute pan at medium heat.

In a food processor, moosh/smoosh/smash/obliterate everything except for the first four ingredients listed above (the raw crust, oil, shredded cheese and TVP). Pour the gloop form the food processor into a mixing bowl, and stir the TVP into it.

Preheat the oven to 375°F/190°C (sometime during the next step).

Transfer this mushy stuff to the large deep saute pan and cook covered for ~15 minutes, lifting the cover to stir regularly. Remember, there's raw onion, pepper and mushroom in there and we want those molecular components cooked! You want to cook this until excess water evaporates, leaving you with a filling you can use immediately.

Brush all of this onto the top layer of the phyllo dough crust.

Salt and pepper to taste, top with the shredded cheese, roll it up like a carpet roll, and bake for 15 minutes on a parchment paper lined baking sheet.

Because this dish uses the cooking spray method on the phyllo dough—instead of melted margarine or olive oil—it is much lower in fat since cooking spreay bottles typically boast 0 calories! But the phyllo dough will still react appropriately making this a great lower fat alternative.

Cream Sauce Pizzas

Follow the general steps for preparing the phyllo dough pizza crust—either using the melted margarine, oil or cooking spray method, with the raw phyllo crust organized on a large baking sheet lined with parchment paper.

For the cream sauce, make the Creamy Pasta and Pizza Sauce (in the Pasta & Sauces section). Cream sauce is great for activating your inner Jackson Pollock since it's so easy to splash and spread around with a silicon brush.

Now let's come up with some topping combos!

<u>The Polo Marco</u>
Since I already have a Marco Polo recipe (the eggplant panini), let's just flip those two words around for this one, which admittedly is confusing because variants of 'pollo' mean chicken in different languages but that's also a white protein which this pizza has plenty of.

On top of the cream-sauce brushed uncooked phyllo dough crust, lay out:

Scissor-cut slivers of the marinated baked tofu slices (see the Protein section)
Sundried tomatoes
Fresh cut parsley
Sauteed shallot slices (prepared in advance)

Bake at 375°F/190°C for 15 minutes.

Right out of the oven, drizzle with the Balsamic Reduction which should be at room temperature (see the next recipe after the topping ideas).

<u>The Crunchy Hamburger</u>
This recipe uses rehydrated TVP to affect ground beef texture and protein content. And to make it crunchy, why not pumpkin seeds?

On top of the cream-sauce brushed uncooked phyllo dough crust, lay out:

Sprinkled rehydrated TVP
Sprinkled pumpkin seeds
Some salad greens, such as spring mix, baby spinach or a 50/50 mix
Sauteed shallot slices (prepared in advance)

Bake at 375°F/190°C for 15 minutes.

Right out of the oven, drizzle with the Balsamic Reduction which should be at room temperature (see the next recipe), because you should always have some left over balsamic reduction so may as well use it!

<u>The Confused Sloppy Joe</u>

Usually there are cream sauce pizza bases, and tomato sauce pizza bases, and never the meet shall twain. Not with this recipe! We're going to get all confusionosity with this topping.

In a medium-sized mixing bowl, combine 2 cups of the Marinara Sauce (see the recipe in the Pasta section) with 2 cups of rehydrated TVP and ½ cup hot red pepper paste (this last ingredient can usually be found at a Middle Eastern grocery store). This is our sloppy joe.

On top of the cream-sauce brushed uncooked phyllo dough crust, lay out the sloppy joe, sprinkle some capers on top of that (I prefer the smaller kind), some soft boiled garlic cloves and that's it!

Bake at 375°F/190°C for 15 minutes.

Balsamic Reduction

1 cup balsamic vinegar (lowest carb option you can find
3 tbsp monk fruit or stevia
½ tsp Dijon mustard (optional, for added flavor)
Pinch of salt

In a small saucepan, combine the balsamic vinegar and low-carb sweetener. Add the pinch of salt. Place the saucepan over medium heat and bring the mixture to a simmer. Stir occasionally to dissolve the sweetener.

Once it starts simmering, reduce the heat to low to maintain a gentle simmer. Simmer the mixture for ~20 minutes, stirring occasionally to prevent burning. I like to bring it up to a foamy froth for a few moments towards the end, to ensure it's going to be thick enough.

If you like, add Dijon mustard to the glaze during the last few minutes of simmering for an extra layer of flavor. Stir well.

Allow the balsamic glaze to cool before using. It will continue to thicken as it cools. Once cooled, transfer it to a container and store it in the refrigerator.

Pulp Pizza Crust

As someone who has both lived in Chicago and eaten pizza in Naples—where pizza was invented— I can attest that some pizzas are best eaten with a fork and spoon, and not handheld in the American-in-a-rush style. The pulp crust pizza is in this more polite sit down tradition even though it is technically possible to eat it with your fingers.

If you want to get a perfectly circular shape out of this dough, simply take one of your pots or pans with the vertical edges of the desired diameter, turn it upside down and, you guessed it, press down hard and eliminate all the extra bits that remain outside the circular edge.

2 cups broccoli and cauliflower pulp (combined)
1 flax egg (1 tbsp ground flax seed & 3 tbsp water)
¼ cup coconut (or almond) flour
¼ cup nutritional yeast
1 tsp baking powder
½ tsp garlic powder
½ tsp onion powder
½ tsp dried oregano
Salt and pepper to taste

Thaw two packages (as these are usually sold separately) of frozen cauliflower and broccoli, ~ 1 bag of ~800g each.

Preheat the oven to 375°F/190°C.

Make a flax egg by mixing 1 tbsp ground flax seed with 3 tbsp water in a small bowl. Let sit for at least 5 minutes.

Using a juicer, juice the cauliflower and broccoli, and move the pulp to a large mixing bowl (the juice is the basis of the Pizza Penance recipe in the Drinks section). Add the flax egg and all remaining ingredients to the pulp and knead into a 'doughy enough' consistency and make a ball out of it.

On a parchment paper lined pizza pan, flatten the doughy pulp ball into either a circular or rectangular or if you prefer, a random shape. You will get to a point that if you keep pressing to make it thinner, it will start breaking up, so stop at the point of thickness where it retains its shape, but get it as thin as you reasonably can.

Bake for 30 minutes, then remove it from the oven to add the toppings, and then bake for another 15 minutes.

The Savory Coast

Add the following to the pulp pizza crust after the 30 minute mark (as described above):

Marinara sauce (see the recipe in the Pasta section)
Truffle sauce
Sun-dried tomatoes
Fresh thyme and oregano
Small slices of vegan cheese
Small slices of vegan chorizo

Run the cheese through a mandolin to make thin pieces of it (be careful as cheese is sticky and tricky to work with on a mandolin: use the hand protector, as you always should, incidentally, when slicing with this tool). The chorizo is easy to cut with scissors.

Brush the marinara sauce over the crust. Make little dollops of the truffle sauce with a small spoon here and there across the crust, and then brush it into the marinara sauce in artsy dark swirls. Arrange the slices of cheese, chorizo and pieces of sun-dried tomatoes into an arrangement that you like, and top with the fresh herbs. Bake for another 15 minutes.

This pizza is savory! And should remind you of the Mediterranean coast.

<u>Rorschach Flatbread</u>

This flatbread goes against the idea of 'don't play with your food."

Take whatever pulp you have left after making a pulp crust pizza, and make a new dough ball out of it. Follow the same general steps of making a pulp crust, but scale the ingredients to the amount of pulp you have left.

Then, shape the dough into a very random and yet symmetrical shape on the parchment paper lining the pizza pan. The trick is to try to make the shape symmetrical while also making it as blobby and random as possible. Stop when you achieve a shape that triggers neurotic mental associations.

After baking for 30 minutes, top it with whatever you feel like, or with whatever you associate with its Rorschackian shape, then bake for another 15 minutes.

Savory Pancake

And you thought potato pancakes were filling! And you never knew that a pancake recipe could go into the Pizza section of a cookbook.

The Savory Pancake is made with the same process as the Pulp Pizza Crust above (reference that recipe to make the batter for this one), only a) you're going to pan fry it instead, and b) you're going to change up the ingredients, which can be anything that generates pulp but for this recipe, let's switch out the broccoli and cauliflower for:

Zucchini
Green bell peppers
2 tbsp garlic (or other) flavored extra virgin olive oil
1 tsp grated vegan parmesan cheese per small pancake

Makes many servings, depending on how large you make the pancakes, or how much pulp you need to turn into pancakes.

Keep the juice! It is the basis of the Pancake Penance recipe in the Drinks section.

Heat the oil in a skillet at medium low heat.

Remove any long unpulped pieces that were too stubborn to get juiced properly from the batter. Sculpt the batter into smaller balls and from there, into smaller discs that roughly resemble a pancake. Place them into the skillet one at a time, and immediately scooch it around and flip over with the spatula, so that the oil evenly coats both sides right away (otherwise one side will absorb too much of the oil too fast).

Use the spatula to smoosh the pancake to a reasonable thickness. Cook on the skillet until browned enough and it makes you think it's a pancake, ~5 minutes per cake. As a final flourish, add the grated vegan parmesan cheese to each side, cooking each side for half a minute to get the cheese heated and settled into the surface. Alternatively, you can mix the grated parmesan cheese into the batter itself so that its taste carries through the whole pancake, rather than treating it as a surface phenomenon.

If your first pancakes don't hold their round shape (as you get used to varying the ratios to your heat levels etc.), that's ok. Just treat them more like green hash browns, as they are still yummy. As they say in the comics, "Hulk smash green eggs and ham!"

Do not smother sour cream or maple syrup on top of them, as that would defeat the point of making these.

Pizza Topping Ideas

Here are some ideas you can try for making interesting toppings to your low carb vegan pizzas.

Mexican
Vegan cheese (nondairy, low-carb option)
Avocado slices or guacamole
Salsa (sugar-free)
Black olives
Jalapeño slices
Red or green bell pepper strips
Red onion slices
Cherry tomatoes or grape tomatoes, halved
Cilantro leaves
Vegan chorizo crumbles
Lime wedges (for squeezing over the pizza after baking)

Thai
Vegan peanut sauce (sugar-free)
Tofu cubes or crumbles, marinated with Thai spices
Sliced bell peppers (red, yellow, or green)
Bean sprouts
Broccoli or broccoli rabe
Sliced red onion
Sliced mushrooms
Thai basil leaves
Lime wedges (for squeezing over the pizza after baking)
Crushed peanuts or cashews
Sriracha or chili sauce (sugar-free)

French
Vegan béchamel sauce
Sautéed mushrooms (with garlic and herbs)
Caramelized onions
Vegan Gruyère or Swiss-style cheese
Fresh thyme leaves
Dijon mustard drizzle
Artichoke hearts
Vegan ham or seitan slices

Spinach or arugula
Capers
Vegan parmesan

Indian

Vegan tikka masala sauce (sugar-free)
Cauliflower florets, roasted with Indian spices
Spinach or kale leaves
Sliced bell peppers (red, yellow, or green)
Red onion slices
Cherry tomatoes or grape tomatoes, halved
Vegan paneer
Cilantro leaves
Sliced green chilies
Garam masala or curry powder sprinkle
Cashew cream drizzle (made with blended cashews and water)
Vegan mozzarella or non-dairy cheese

Middle Eastern

Baba ganoush or hummus spread (as the pizza sauce)
Sliced cherry tomatoes or grape tomatoes
Sliced cucumber
Kalamata olives, sliced
Red onion slices
Artichoke hearts
Spinach or arugula leaves
Vegan feta or tofu feta crumbles
Za'atar seasoning sprinkle
Fresh mint leaves
Drizzle of tahini sauce or vegan tzatziki
Sumac sprinkle

Greek

Vegan tzatziki sauce (cucumber and garlic yogurt)
Kalamata olives, sliced
Sliced cherry tomatoes or grape tomatoes
Red onion slices
Spinach or arugula leaves
Artichoke hearts
Vegan feta or tofu feta crumbles
Sliced cucumber

Fresh oregano leaves
Drizzle of extra virgin olive oil
Lemon wedges (for squeezing over the pizza after baking)
Pepperoncini slices for some heat

Chinese
Hoisin sauce or low-carb hoisin alternative (sugar-free)
Sliced shiitake mushrooms
Water chestnuts, sliced
Bok choy or baby bok choy, chopped
Sliced bell peppers (red, yellow, or green)
Scallions (green onions), sliced
Vegan chicken or tofu, marinated with soy sauce and ginger
Sesame seeds, toasted
Fresh cilantro leaves
Sliced garlic
Ginger, grated or sliced
Chili oil (optional, for heat)

Africa
Harissa or African spice-infused tomato sauce (sugar-free)
Sliced okra
Sliced bell peppers (red, yellow, or green)
Red onion slices
Cherry tomatoes or grape tomatoes, halved
Spinach or kale leaves
Vegan feta or tofu feta crumbles
Sliced black olives
Plantains, sliced and grilled
Peanut sauce drizzle
Berbere spice sprinkle (for heat, an Ethiopian spice blend)
Fresh cilantro or parsley leaves

South America
Chimichurri sauce or salsa verde (as the pizza sauce)
Black beans, cooked (not too many, as they are high in carbs)
Sliced cherry tomatoes or grape tomatoes
Avocado slices or guacamole
Red onion slices
Sliced bell peppers (red, yellow, or green)
Jalapeño slices

Vegan chorizo crumbles
Corn kernels (just a few, as they are high in carbs)
Vegan cheese
Cilantro leaves
Lime wedges (for squeezing over the pizza after baking)

Pacific Islands

Coconut milk or coconut cream-based sauce (as the pizza sauce)
Pineapple chunks or rings (sparingly, as they are high in carbs)
Sliced red or yellow bell peppers
Red onion slices
Sliced cherry tomatoes or grape tomatoes
Shiitake mushrooms, sliced
Baby spinach leaves
Macadamia nuts, chopped
Vegan bacon or coconut flakes
Vegan cheese
Fresh cilantro leaves
Lime wedges (for squeezing over the pizza after baking)

Pacific Northwest

Vegan pesto or garlic-infused olive oil (as the pizza sauce)
Wild mushrooms, such as chanterelles or morels, sautéed with garlic
Baby spinach or arugula leaves
Sliced cherry tomatoes or grape tomatoes
Red onion slices
Vegan cheese
Hazelnuts, chopped
Smoked tofu or tempeh, crumbled or sliced
Dill or tarragon leaves
Vegan cream cheese or cashew cream drizzle
Lemon zest or a squeeze of fresh lemon juice

Korean

Gochujang-infused tomato or barbecue sauce (as the pizza sauce)
Sliced shiitake mushrooms, marinated in soy sauce and sesame oil
Sliced red or yellow bell peppers
Vegan Kimchi
Vegan bulgogi-style crumbles (using TVP or tempeh)
Baby spinach or arugula leaves

Sliced green onions
Sesame seeds, toasted
Vegan cheese
Drizzle of sesame oil or chili oil for extra flavor
Nori (seaweed) flakes or strips

Rices

Paella

1 package konjac rice, 398g
1 tsp refined avocado oil
1 tbsp garlic flavored extra virgin olive oil
Saffron (1 small pinch suffices)
2 tbsp ajvar (a red pepper spread)
1 tbsp tomato paste
1 link of (store bought) seitan paprika sausage, 88g

Makes 1-2 servings (this depends on how hungry you are, or if someone is eyeing you over the shoulder wanting some, too).

Preheat the oven to 395°F/202°C. These might seem like strange numbers, but due to the use of premium extra virgin olive oil, which has a smoking point of 410°, I sometimes like to give myself a little padding and not go right up to the edge with the temperature. This temperature is certainly close enough!

Coat a small (~6" x 9"/15cm x 23cm) casserole dish with the avocado oil. Since avocado oil has a smoking point of 520°F/271°C, it works great for coating baking dishes so that food doesn't stick to them too much during cleaning. This oil can really handle the heat! Premium extra virgin olive oil will also work, but because I am using the more expensive flavored kind in the paella, I use avocado oil for mainly nonstick purposes here.

Drain the water out of the konjac rice package and transfer the konjac to a mixing bowl. Mix in the saffron (a small finger pinch is sufficient to get the flavor), the olive oil, ajvar and tomato paste. Stir. Cut the seitan paprika sausage into thin slices and stir into the mix.

Transfer all this into the small casserole dish and bake for 20 minutes, and that's it! Eat while hot, and dream of Spain.

Red Curry Rice and Tofu

1 ½ cups cooked riced cauliflower
6 tbsp red curry paste
2 cups coconut milk (the kind used for drinking or adding to
coffee, not the thicker canned kind for cooking)
4-6 slices of the baked marinated tofu, cut into smaller pieces
1 tbsp ajvar
Fresh basil

Variation: try other curry pastes!

Makes 4 servings (the sauce does, the servings for the rice portion
depends on the size of your cauliflower rice package).

This recipe uses the drinkable coconut milk, usually sold in the
dairy section with the non dairy milks, not the canned coconut milk
sold in the aisles in the "Asian Food" section (which is where you
find the red curry paste). Canned coconut milk has a lot more
coconut cream (and thus more fat and calories) compared to the
drinkable variety, which still works as a healthier curry sauce.

Prepare a package of riced cauliflower, and transfer ~1 ½ cups to a
bowl. Heat the coconut milk on low heat, and stir in the red curry
paste and ajvar. Red curry often has red peppers, and ajvar is a fast
and easy, kinda lazy gourmet method for imparting red pepper
flavor to this dish without the red pepper carbs (of the bell
peppers, red has the highest carb count).

While making the sauce, warm the tofu slices (it's a good idea to
just always have cooked marinated tofu slices in the fridge, for
fast access to dishes). Place the tofu on the rice, then pour a half
cup of the sauce into the bowl, stir a bit, and top with the fresh
basil.

Coconut Rice

This dish is inspired by my travels to the Lamu Archipelago off the east coast of Kenya, a magical and inspiring environment and culture.

1 cup ground coconut flakes
1 tbsp flavored extra virgin olive oil (I like green chili infused)
1 large onion
A dozen cooked garlic cloves
1 heaping tbsp of Super Spice (see the recipe in the Panty Stocking section)
1 cup coconut milk (the lighter kind for drinking and coffee)
500g cooked riced cauliflower

Makes 4-6 servings.

Variation: use coconut oil instead of olive oil, if you crave more saturated fats in your diet.

Preheat the oven to 325°F/163°C.

On a flat baking sheet or pizza pan lined with parchment paper, spread out the ground coconut flakes evenly and bake for ~5 minutes until light brown, nicely golden or Pantone 18-1029 Tpx Toasted Coconut Color #916f56.

You can toast as much ground coconut as you want, as this is a handy dry ingredient that will last a while and you can use it in other dishes or just tell visitors, "Hey, know what? I toasted this coconut myself!"

In a large sauté pan with tall sides, add the olive oil and heat at low or high simmer heat.

Because I like to do things fast and lazy, I always make my coconut rice just after I've made my weekly vegetable broth, because I can immediately use the cooked onion and garlic cloves in this recipe. If you are less lazy, then sauté chopped onion until soft and translucent, adding minced garlic towards the end of the onion softening so it doesn't overcook.

After ~1 minute using my lazy method (or ~10 minutes if you're working harder), add the Super Spice and cook for ~1 minute so the spices start to release their flavor. Whether working lazy or non-lazily, make sure to thoroughly stir the onions and garlic in the olive oil to get the flavor, and also stir after adding the spice.

Add the coconut milk (remember, this is the lighter drinkable kind), stir and bring to a simmer for 2-3 minutes, then add in the cooked riced cauliflower. Simmer for ~8-10 minutes while the cooked riced cauliflower cooks a bit more in the simmering spiced coconut milk mixture.

Add in a heaping tbsp of the toasted ground coconut, which will absorb some of the liquid and make the rice less saucy. Stir for half a minute or so and you're done. Garnish the rice in the bowls with some more toasted coconut on top. For a complete meal, top with heated baked marinated tofu slices (see the recipe in the Proteins section).

Kimchi Fried Rice

1 package konjac rice, 398g
1 tbsp chili (or other) flavored extra virgin olive oil
2 cups scissors cut vegan kimchi

Makes 2 servings.

In a large skillet or sauté pan, heat the oil at medium heat. Add the konjac rice and cut up kimchi, stir thoroughly and cook for ~8 minutes. Konjac has a lot of water content and so the dish doesn't need a lot of oil to cook, but it does take awhile to release the water. Since I cook on nonstick surfaces, I don't use high heat. Stir occasionally because it can be surprising how suddenly the mix starts to stick to the pan. Cook and stir until the mixture takes on a dryness and consistency that reminds you of regular fried rice!

Risotto

1 tbsp garlic flavored extra virgin olive oil
1 package konjac rice
1 tsp onion powder
1 tsp dried basil
1 tbsp minced garlic
⅓ cup grated parmesan cheese
¼ cup warm vegetable broth
¼ cup unsweetened cashew milk
Salt and pepper to taste
Fresh herbs if desired

For a more rice-like texture, dry bake the konjac rice for 15 minutes at 350°F/177°C on a parchment lined baking sheet (this is optional, and discussed in the intro section on Konjac).

Heat the oil at low or high simmer heat (lower than Low on my stove, which has High and Low Simmer notches past the Low setting, so this depends on your range top). Add the onion powder, basil and minced garlic and stir everything together with a silicon brush.

When you start to see little bubbles, add the konjac rice and stir everything thoroughly to make sure the konjac rice is well coated with the mixture. Cook for 2 minutes. Add the salt and pepper, stir again, then add ¼ cup of the warm vegetable broth. Cook for 10 minutes, stirring occasionally, then add ¼ cup cashew milk, cook and stir for another 10 minutes.

Don't worry if it looks a little liquidy because you will need that fluid to help melt the cheese. Add the grated vegan parmesan cheese, stir it in thoroughly and cook until it melts into a creamy coating, in around 5 minutes. It's ok to cheat a little and strain the risotto before you place it in bowls, if you have any residual wateriness you don't like. Since you're not using Arborio rice, you can be forgiven. Garnish with some fresh herbs if desired, and serve.

Dill Rice

1 package konjac rice, 398g
1 tbsp garlic flavored extra virgin olive oil (drizzle to taste)
1 tbsp fresh scissored dill pieces
A pinch of saffron

Rinse and heat the konjac rice in the microwave for 90 seconds on high. Toss with the olive oil, add the dill and saffron, and toss some more to evenly coat the rice with oil, saffron and dill. That's it, super easy.

Spanish Rice

1 cup prepared riced cauliflower
½ cup of the Marinara Sauce (see the recipe in the Pasta section)
Garlic flavored extra virgin olive oil (drizzle to taste)

Mix the warmed up marinara sauce into the heated cauliflower rice, drizzle with the olive oil, and serve—that's it! Add some fresh herbs if so inspired.

Protein

Marinated Tofu Slices

1 block of medium or extra firm tofu
Flavored extra virgin olive oil

The harder the tofu, the less it tends to absorb the flavors of a marinade. I often like working with extra firm tofu because it holds its shape well, but a medium tofu will take in more marinade, so your choice!

If working with a firm or extra firm tofu, it's usually recommended to press it, whereby you wrap the tofu in a kitchen towel or some paper towels, put it on a plate, then put a weight on top of it for half an hour.

I like marinating tofu slices overnight in a garlic or chili flavored extra virgin olive oil. Then, I either bake or saute it to add it to my veggies.

Cedar Baked Tofu

All the slices from 1 block of medium or extra firm marinated tofu (see the discussion above on marinating tofu)
1 cedar plank for cooking

Makes 2-4 servings (it kinda depends on how much tofu you want to eat :)

Soak a cedar plank (sold for cooking) for 2 hours in water.

Preheat the oven to 400°F/205°C. When the temperature is achieved, place the cedar plank in the oven, so it starts to let off steam and flavor. The cedar will impart some of its smokey and woodsy flavor to the tofu.

Add the tofu slices to the plank, and bake for 20-25 minutes, or until you reach your desired level of browning and crispiness. The tofu can be eaten as it, put onto a salad, placed on top of cold or sautéed kimchi, and can generally be treated as a source of handy sliced and well-flavored protein. Just a reminder—it's really great on top of the coconut rice!

Because the pleasures of food involve the nose as much as the mouth, I like to keep the cedar plank close by on the table, so I continue to take in its ambient aroma during my meal. It can even seem a bit like you're eating inside a Swedish sauna or something! The cedar planks can be used a few times. I use mine twice, flipping it over to use the unused other side the second time, before discarding it in the green bin.

Seitan

1½ cup vital wheat gluten
¼ cup nutritional yeast
1 tsp garlic powder
1 tsp onion powder
½ tsp smoked paprika (optional, for flavor)
1 cup vegetable broth or water
2 tbsp soy sauce or tamari
1 tbsp olive oil
Additional vegetable broth for the long simmer

Made from Gwyneth Paltrow's arch nemesis wheat gluten, seitan is not for the gluten intolerant.

In a mixing bowl, combine the dry ingredients: vital wheat gluten, nutritional yeast, garlic powder, onion powder and smoked paprika.

In a separate bowl, whisk the wet ingredients: vegetable broth, soy sauce (or tamari), and olive oil.

Pour the wet ingredients into the dry ingredients and stir until it forms a dough. Knead the dough for ~3 minutes until it becomes elastic. You can do this in the bowl or on a clean surface. As you knead it, seek out with your fingertips any tiny hard granules that have congealed, and simply remove them.

Shape the seitan into a log or cut it into smaller pieces, depending on your preference. Simmer in vegetable broth for one hour (note that the seitan will enlarge as it cooks).

Place the cooked seitan on a plate with raised edges, and place another plate on top of it, and press to squeeze excess water out. Once cooled, the seitan is ready to be used in various dishes—sliced, cubed, chopped, shredded—and however you wish to use a meaty texture.

Extra Lazy Cooking Method

This might sound like seitanic heresy, but you can completely omit the presence of vegetable broth in the recipe, and use just plain ol' water instead. You can add flavor to the seitan through marinating instead (discussed below in the next section) and of course, by sauteeing it or pouring a sauce on top!

Seitan Marinades

For baking, grilling, panini-ing, stir frying, and whatever else you can think of doing with 'wheat meat,' marinating seitan slices will add a lot of flavor. Adding seitan to a salad, vegetable or rice will make it into a complete meal. Marinate for 1-24 hours, depending on how much time you have for marinating.

Here are some simple low carb marinades to try (experiment with your own ratios to taste):

Marinade #1: Lemon Herb Olive Oil Marinade

Lemon juice
Olive oil
Fresh herbs (rosemary, thyme or oregano)
Garlic (minced)
Salt and pepper

Marinade #2: Mustard and Herb Marinade
Dijon mustard
Apple cider vinegar
Fresh or dried herbs (rosemary, thyme or oregano)
Garlic (minced)
Salt and pepper

Marinade #3: Herb-infused Vinegar Marinade
Red wine vinegar or white wine vinegar
Fresh or dried herbs (basil, thyme, rosemary)
Garlic (minced)
Salt and pepper

Marinade #4: Spicy Lime Cilantro Marinade
Lime juice
Olive oil
Cilantro (chopped)
Jalapeño (minced)
Cumin
Salt and pepper

Marinade #5: Sesame and Tamari Marinade
Toasted sesame oil
Tamari
Rice vinegar
Garlic (minced)
Sesame seeds

Marinade #6: Garlic and Herb Marinade
Olive oil
Garlic (minced)
Fresh or dried herbs (thyme, rosemary, or oregano)
Salt and pepper

Marinade #7: Cilantro Lime Avocado Oil Marinade
Avocado oil
Lime juice
Cilantro (chopped)
Garlic (minced)
Salt and pepper

Whisky Barrel Plank Baked Marinated Seitan

And you thought cedar planks were fancy? Based on a web search, there appears to be only one producer of whisky barrel planks for grilling, Crown Royal, which makes a Canadian blended whisky here in Canada no less (where I live). When rats chew through the whisky barrels, the company removes the spoiled planks and sells them for home grilling. Just kidding.

Preheat your oven to 375°F/190.556°C.

Arrange a number of marinated seitan slices onto the whisky barrel plank, and bake for 25-30 minutes. Place the plank on a middle rack in your oven, and below that, place a baking sheet to catch any drippings from the marinade if using a wet one.

When served, keep the seitan on the plank and make sure everyone knows that these have been cooked on genuine whisky barrel planks. If you are quizzed further, note that the wood is American Oak. If you are quizzed further than that, tell people that you know someone at Crown Royal who sneaks these out for you personally, after hours.

Oh, and eat with single malt Scotch, not Canadian whisky.

One cool thing about baking on wooden planks is that there's no surface to clean up afterwards, nothing to scrub or cycle through the dishwasher. Thus, using wood as a baking surface can become addictive if you hate washing dishes. Remember to send these planks on their way to the composting green bin when you've used them for the recommended number of times stated on the package.

Grandmas' Grave Cutlet

No, this recipe name is not meant to suggest that the dish will send you into early retirement. Rather, I imagine this vegan version of one of my favorite Eastern European meat dishes—the pan fried cutlet—would have generations of my Polish, Russian and Ukrainian babcias rolling in their graves, or at least rolling their eyes, if they had eyes of course (hence the placement of the apostrophe in the name of this dish).

I think they would object to a) the lack of meat in this cutlet and b) the decisively non-Eastern European spices (if following this recipe to a T, which is still a T even in Cyrillic!). You can of course spice it how you like.

2 tbsp avocado oil
2 cups of the refried black soy bean taco filling (see the Chickpea Flour Soft Tacos in the Protein + Veggie section)
½ cup almond flour
½ cup sauteed finely chopped onions
½ cup mushrooms (any kind), pulverized in a food processor
Salt and pepper to taste

Makes 2 cutlets aka 2 servings

Have a batch of the refried black soy bean filling from the Chickpea Flour Soft Taco recipe already made, but without the mushroom option in that recipe.

Heat 1 tbsp of the avocado oil in a small skillet at low heat. Finely chop a small onion (or half a medium one) and add it to the skillet. Halve or quarter the mushrooms—I like brown cremini for this—and make a mush out of it in a food processor. Add the mushrooms to the onions and stir, sauteing and stirring regularly until the onions are soft. Place in a bowl to cool.

Heat the other tbsp of avocado oil in another small or medium sized skillet.

Pour the almond flour on a large plate and distribute it evenly across it. With one hand, grab an almost cutlet-sized chunk of the refried black soybeans, and with another hand, grab a bit of the cooled mushroom and onion mix. With your third hand, set the timer for, oh wait, sorry, wrong planet (this cookbook is also sold in other solar systems).

With your two human hands, smoosh the refried beans mixture into the mushroom and onion mixture, making a new composite mixture into a ball shape. You can of course do this in a more civilized way, by combining these two substances in a mixing bowl with a DJ mix wand, but I never outgrew playing with my food. Salt and pepper to taste at this stage, or add the S&P on top after it's done frying (I like it that way, actually, which I call "salt and pepper palette forward style." Remember that for the quiz.).

Roll that ball around in circles in the almond flour, to evenly coat the whole surface of the ball and it's ok to roll it around more than you need to because it's kinda fun.

Place the floured ball into the skillet and press down on it with a spatula to make it assume cutlet shape. Cook covered for a few minutes then flip over and do the same. Then, move to a plate, let cool and eat.

You can also pan fry this pancake style, if you want to impress people with your strange breakfast ideas.

You may want to omit the onion and mushroom component of this recipe, which will simply yield a drier cutlet without the onion and mushroom flavors, but which might work better if you are wanting to eat this more as a burger sandwiched between bun halves.

Burek Roll

You know this dish rocks when your carnivorous dog keeps trying to steal it from you. And it tastes sooooo good with hot sauce!

1 medium onion, finely chopped
2 tbsp extra virgin olive oil, flavored is cool
2 tbsp minced garlic, hand-squeezed to remove excess water
2 cups TVP
Dried herbs (you choose which ones!)
Salt and pepper to taste

Prepare a phyllo dough base of 5-6 layers as described in the Phyllo Pizza Crust recipe in the Pizza section, placed on parchment paper on a baking sheet.

Preheat the oven to 375°F/190°C and dehydrate the TVP aka vegan ground beef according to package directions.

Heat the oil in a large skillet at medium low heat. Sauté the onions with the herbs until they start to get soft. Add the rehydrated TVP (you can adjust the amount to the ratio of herbed onions to your preference), add the minced garlic and keep sautéeing to cook the TVP and marry the flavors. Because TVP never quite looks exactly like ground beef, use the onion softness and translucency to tell you when it's basically done.

Spread the onion-TVP mixture evenly across the top layer of the phyllo dough crust, using a brush to make it smooth, thin, even, geometrical, rectangular etc.

Now, just grab one of the short edges of the phyllo dough crust and roll it up like a carpet. Put this tubular cylindrical log into the oven and bake for 15 minutes.

Let cool, and slice into it. Did I mention it is awesome with hot sauce?

Red Curry and Coconut Sauce

¼ cup ground almonds
¼ cup very hot water
1½ cup leftover red curry sauce (from the Red Curry Rice recipe in the Rice section)
2 tbsp leftover toasted coconut flakes (from the Coconut Rice recipe in the Rice section)
Fresh basil or mint

Variation: thicken with almond flour instead of ground almonds if you don't want the grainy texture.

Makes 6-8 servings.

Soak the ground almonds in the hot water for 1 hour. Pour the leftover red curry sauce into a blender with the ground almond mixture and blend thoroughly. Transfer into a sauce pan, add in the coconut flakes, set heat to low and simmer for 15 minutes, stirring occasionally. As water evaporates, the sauce will thicken. Of course, the almonds and coconut will also thicken it.

The grainy-flaky texture of the almonds and coconut in the sauce contrasts with the slick smoothness of tofu, and thus this is a good sauce to cover baked tofu slices with. Garnish with the fresh basil or mint.

Sesame Ginger Goji Crunch Glaze

2 tbsp tamari or soy sauce (low-sodium)
1 tbsp sesame oil
1 tbsp rice vinegar
1 tbsp strained minced ginger
½ tbsp strained minced garlic
1-2 tsp of stevia or monk fruit (optional, to taste)
Dried goji berries and sunflower seeds, for garnish

Variation: you can garnish with sesame seeds, of course, for a more traditional approach

Makes 4-6 servings.

Minced ginger and garlic can be watery so give them a squeeze—using your fist will do, though hopefully not just after blowing your nose—just squeeze the water out of it hard, that'll do.

Thoroughly whisk together in a mixing bowl the tamari or soy sauce, sesame oil, rice vinegar, ginger and garlic. Sweeten with the monk fruit or stevia if desired (I say go for it). You can add water to thin the glaze—if you need to thicken it, then something has gone terribly wrong—maybe you didn't squeeze the minced garlic and ginger hard enough? Via the whisk stick, get the mixture to a nice smooth and even consistency with your whisking.

Brush or pour onto your protein and garnish with the dried goji fruit and sunflower seeds—my wild radical version—or stick closer to tradition by garnishing with sesame seeds.

This glaze goes well either with the baked seitan or tofu.

Mole Sauce

2 tbsp chili flavored extra virgin olive oil
1 small onion, chopped
1 tbsp minced garlic (strained)
2 tsp ground cumin
2 tsp Super Spice (see the recipe in the Pantry Stocking section)
1 tsp paprika
2 tbsp unsweetened cocoa powder
1 can (14 oz) diced tomatoes, drained
2-3 dried ancho chilies, stemmed and seeded
1 tsp dried oregano
½ tsp ground cinnamon
Salt and pepper to taste
2 cups vegetable broth
1 tbsp ground almonds

Makes 8-10 servings.

Dried ancho chilis are a rather niche ingredient and usually found at Mexican or Latin American grocers, bagged and already dried. With scissors, cut the stems off, cut a slit down one of the sides and remove the seeds. The skins are sticky and it's ok if a few seeds stick to the skin. Toast them in a dry pan over medium low heat for a few minutes until they become fragrant. Soak them in hot water for 20-30 minutes until soft.

In a saucepan, heat 1 tbsp of the chili flavored olive oil over medium heat. Add the chopped onion and minced garlic. Sauté until the onions are soft and translucent. If the onions become translucent while remaining hard, or remain opaque when soft, report the onion species to the FDA as it may be an alien hybrid.

Stir in cumin, Super Spice, paprika and cocoa powder. Add 1 more tbsp of the chili flavored olive oil because once these spices go in, they will soak up what little oil is left. Cook for ~ 1 more minute to toast the spices and cocoa, stirring constantly.

In a blender, combine the sautéed spice mixture, soaked ancho chilies, diced tomatoes, dried oregano, ground cinnamon, salt, and pepper. Blend until the Many become One.

You want to transfer this interesting gloop in the blender over to a saucepan. The problem is, this mixture is very thick and difficult to get out of the container, so you may have to bribe it, just like in Mexico.

Add 1 cup of the vegetable broth and stir well. Add the ground almonds and stir (mole should have a hint of grainy texture, which the almonds provide). Simmer over low heat for ~20 minutes, adding additional water as needed.

If the tomato is too prevalent, counter with additional cocoa, and vice versa. Keep stirring, tasting, countering tomato versus chocolate, adding ground almonds for graininess if needed, and adding water when needed until you cannot resist the urge to yell out Hole Mole! But please do resist.

Cilantro Lime Glaze

1 cup cilantro, chopped
¼ cup fresh lime juice (from 2-3 limes)
1 tbsp minced garlic, squeeze-strained
⅓ cup herb or garlic flavored extra virgin olive oil (such as Tuscan, Milanese Gremolata or Provençal)
Salt and pepper to taste

Makes 8-10 servings of glaze or dollops.

Hand-squeeze the minced garlic to remove excess water. Decide whether you want the olive oil flavoring to accentuate either the garlic or herbs—you must choose one or the other, anything else is wishy washy.

In a blender or food processor, combine the chopped cilantro, lime juice, minced garlic, salt, pepper and olive oil.

Brush, dollop or pour onto seitan, and garnish with, you got it (literally), cilantro! In the photo of the dish, I make a kind of cilantro halo or force field around my seitan with the cilantro garnish (at medium.com/low-carb-vegan on the Proteins page).

Peanut Sauce

½ cup creamy peanut butter
1 tsp minced ginger, squeeze strained
½ tbsp minced garlic, squeeze strained
2 tbsp tamari or soy sauce (low-sodium)
1 tbsp rice vinegar
1 tbsp water
Juice from 1 lime, hand squeezed
1-2 tsp stevia or monk fruit, optional
Super Spice to taste, ~½ - 1 tsp (optional, see the recipe in the Pantry Stocking section)
Garnish with chopped peanuts or cilantro (optional)

Makes 6-8 servings.

The peanut butter will totally stick to whatever measuring instrument you're using, making it rather fascinating, or at least challenging, to figure out how much exactly ½ cup is.

Hand-squeeze the minced garlic and ginger to get the water out, squeezing, like, very hard. When you're done squeezing, it should look like grated or finely chopped treatments.

In a small saucepan at high simmer (or low low) heat, combine and stir the peanut butter, tamari or soy sauce, rice vinegar, lime juice, water, and hand-squeezed minced ginger and garlic. Stir and examine consistency as the peanut butter starts to melt, adding additional water as needed (and it will be needed).

Add stevia or monk fruit to sweeten if desired. Add the Super Spice for more, um, well, spiciness?

Keep stirring, watering, tasting and ingredient adjusting until you get the peanut sauce of your protein enhancing dreams.

Brush or pour over tofu or seitan. Garnish with chopped peanuts or cilantro. This also works as a vegetable dipping sauce. Don't eat if you're allergic to nuts.

Mushroom Gravy

2 cups sliced mushrooms, white or brown or any kind, really
1 small onion, chopped
1½ tbsp minced garlic, hand-squeezed drained of excess water
2 tbsp herb flavored (Tuscan, Milanese or Provençal) extra virgin olive oil
1½ cups vegetable broth
1 tsp dried thyme
1 tsp dried rosemary
2 tbsp almond flour
Salt and pepper to taste
Fresh thyme or rosemary (optional garnish)

Heat the olive oil in a skillet on medium low heat. Add sliced mushrooms and sauté until they release their moisture with a sigh of relief. Add the dried spices, onions and minced garlic to the mushrooms. Sauté until the onions are translucent and the garlic is flagrantly fragrant and aromatic in the ambient atmosphere.

Gradually pour in the vegetable broth in small amounts, and now comes the tricky part. We want to make a sauce with low carb flour and avoid clumpiness or graininess. Pour the flour into the broth very slowly and gradually by placing it into a tea strainer and shaking gently with one hand, while whisking everything together with the other hand. You want to flour to thicken the broth into a gravy, not turn it into liquid sawdust.

As soon as you add some broth and some flour, you'll be like, "Holy sh*asterisk, this is actually like mushroom gravy!" Hold onto that feeling. As they say in Avengers movies, you're in the end game now.

Continue adding broth, whisking and and shaking tea strainer flour slowly until you have the desired gravy consistency. Add salt and pepper to taste. Let it all simmer for a while, as you visually examine the chemical reactions and consistency transformations. Continue to add the broth, but if it gets too watery, add some more flour. It's now a battle of broth versus flour in the thickening end game.

Garnish with fresh thyme or rosemary if you'd like to, and pour over your protein, such as baked seitan.

By the way, placing fresh herbs in a tea strainer and running them under the faucet is also how I wash them, since they are much easier to separate from the stems when dry than wet.

Buffalo Sauce

1 cup vegan vegetable margarine spread
1 cup hot sauce (low-carb variety, as high up the Scoville scale as you dare)
1 tbsp vegan Worcestershire sauce substitute
1 tsp garlic powder
½ tsp onion powder

Makes 10-12 servings as a protein topper, depending on the size of the buffalo sauce craving.

Variation or handy tip: since it's usually easier to find very large bottles of hot sauce in the milder flavors. If you want more heat, just add small amounts of a very hot hot sauce (like, XXX Haberno etc.) which is usually sold in more expensive and smaller bottles.

In a saucepan at low heat, melt the margarine. With a silicon brush, stir in the hot sauce, mixing it well with the melted margarine, then add the vegan Worcestershire sauce.

Regular Worcestershire sauce has anchovies in it, so regrettably it is not vegan, but there are companies that sell a vegan version. If you can't find a vegan Worcestershire sauce, you can make a simple substitute by combining soy sauce, apple cider vinegar, a dash of stevia or monk fruit, and a pinch of cloves (adjusting ratios to taste).

Mix in the garlic and onion powder and keep stirring. Taste and check to see if salt is needed but usually it's not. Simmer for ~5 minutes, stirring occasionally. Add water to thicken if needed. Adjust to taste: more hot sauce for heat, more Worcestershire for depth, but be careful because too much Worcestershire can add a sour taste.

This works well as a sauce or marinade for tofu or seitan, or as a coating as used in the Buffalo Cauliflower Bombs recipe in the Veggies section.

Garnish with rattlesnake venom. Actually, don't.

Veggies

Soft Boiled Garlic Cloves

If you buy already peeled garlic cloves in bulk, get in the habit of boiling a bunch and keeping them in the fridge, since they have so many uses. Just give them a rinse and drop them in a pot of boiling water for 15 minutes, then store in a container.

These are a great alternative to minced garlic (which is often very watery) or garlic powder (which often explodes in a dust storm all over your shirt). Also, when soft, they are so easy to chop into smaller pieces and won't go flying across your countertop every time your knife slices into them.

They work well in sauces, such as my Creamy Alfredo Sauce (see the recipe in the Pastas section), or as simple snacks, just laying on top of marinated baked tofu (see the recipe in the Protein section).

Or, make toothpick mini skewers, stacking olives, garlic, cherry tomatoes and whatever else will fit on a toothpick when you are looking for snacky things to eat.

Roasted Green Beans and Shallots

Did you know that green beans aren't beans? With this veggie, we eat the unripe young fruit that has yet to mature into full blown beans. They are more like 'someday beans' but since they are green, they're name isn't a total falsehood. Rest assured, though, that they are still legumes, but no one wants to call them 'baby green legumes,' presumably.

It's this developmental (not mental) immaturity that makes green beans so low carb. If their beans-to-be were, well, beans, then they would be loaded with carbs in the way that most beans are. Green beans quite literally nip carbs in the bud, by nipping them at baby bean stage.

These legume younglings are rich in vitamins K and C, as well as iron, folate, manganese, antioxidants, some good ol' protein, fiber of course (that's a no brainer), and *quercetin*, which is a flavonoid with senolytic effects, since it helps the body eliminate zombie cells ! Woo hoo, you can kill zombies eating this stuff! That's also a no brainer (there's some kind of missing joke here, about zombies and brains.). Aren't you glad I don't try to be funny with every recipe in this book?

Now that you have a thorough scientific understanding of green beans, here's one low carb vegan way you can eat them fast and easy.

A bag of trimmed green beans (~680g)
3 whole shallots
2 tbsp herb flavored extra virgin olive oil (Tuscan, Milanese Gremolata or Provençal)
2 tbsp grapefruit (or other citrus) flavored white balsamic vinegar
Salt and pepper to taste

Makes 6 servings.

Preheat the oven to 400°F/205°C.

Put swimming goggles on so that cutting the shallots doesn't burn your eyes. Always remember to wear swimming goggles when cutting, chopping or dicing any member of the onion family. If you also need reading glasses to read this recipe while slicing shallots, you can get prescription swimming goggles.

Slice the shallots into small pieces and combine with the green beans in a mixing bowl. In a separate bowl, whisk the oil and vinegar, then pour onto the green beans and shallots. Toss and add salt and pepper to taste.

Line a large baking sheet with parchment paper and spread the green bean and shallot mixture evenly across it. Roast in the oven for 40 minutes.

Green Bean Casserole

A low carb vegan take on a classic comfort food, and senolytic side dish for the ages.

Casserole:
1 ½ pound fresh green beans, trimmed and cut into bite-sized pieces
2 tbsp extra virgin olive oil
1 medium onion, finely chopped or mechanically minced
5 cloves garlic, minced
1 ½ cups sliced mushrooms (any kind, I won't tell)

Sauce:
1 cup nondairy milk, consider cashew milk
1 package silken tofu, ~400g
3 tbsp nutritional yeast
3 tbsp Dijon mustard
Salt and pepper to taste

Topping:
2 cups crispy fried onions (store bought)
3 tbsp nutritional yeast
3 tbsp extra virgin olive oil (consider chili flavored for a touch of kick)

Makes 8 servings.

Preheat the oven to 375°F (190°C).

Bring a large pot of salted water to a boil. Add the green beans and cook for ~3 minutes until they are bright green, almost glowing with green bean radiation. With a slotted spoon or skimming ladle, transfer right away to a large bowl of ice water to stop the cooking process. Drain and set aside.

For the onions and garlic, you may work hard using your finely chopping knife skills, or throw them both into a small food processor and grind into a slurry. Either way works since we're making a casserole! To be honest, when I'm feeling lazy, I sometimes thrown the mushrooms into the processor to, if you do the same, ignore the mushroom instructions in the next paragraph:

In a large skillet, heat 2 tbsp of olive oil over medium heat. Add the onions and garlic and sauté until softened. Add sliced mushrooms and cook until they release their water without breaking a sweat.

In a blender, combine the nondairy milk, nutritional yeast, Dijon mustard, salt and pepper until nice and creamy. You can thin the sauce with more nondairy milk if desired. Add this sauce to the large skillet and simmer for ~10 minutes until the sauce thickens slightly.

Add the blanched green beans to the skillet and toss until the green beans are coated with the sauce. Transfer the mixture to a greased casserole dish.

In a small bowl, combine the fried onions, nutritional yeast and olive oil. Mix until well combined, and add to the top of the casserole, spreading it out evenly.

Bake for exactly approximately ~25-30 minutes. Perhaps the topping will be golden brown and the casserole bubbling :)

Creamed Baked Kalettes

Kalettes are a new vegetable invented by hybridizing kale with the Frankenstein CRISPR genes of Brussel sprouts (which always insist on being capitalized in a spell checker) in a radioactive chamber managed by genetically modified organism cyborg engineers. So, you may as well eat them. They look like baby kale mushrooms but have the charming tooth pickable size of their Brussel sprouts heritage.

1 lb kalettes (16oz / 454g), washed of course
3 tbsp extra virgin olive oil
4 cloves garlic, minced
1 cup unsweetened almond milk (or any nondairy milk)
1 package of silken tofu
2 tbsp nutritional yeast
1 tbsp lemon juice
1 tsp Dijon mustard
Salt and pepper to taste

Makes 8 servings.

Wash the kalettes. Bring a pot of water to a boil and blanch the kalettes for 2-3 minutes. Drain and set aside.

Preheat the oven to 375°F (190°C).

In a blender, combine the silken tofu, the almond milk, nutritional yeast, lemon juice, Dijon mustard, salt and pepper. Blend until smooth and creamy. If the sauce is too thick, you can add a bit more nondairy milk.

In a *very* large skillet or alternatively a big pot, heat the olive oil over medium heat. Add the minced garlic and sauté for 1-2 minutes until fragrant, which means the air smells like garlic.

Add the blanched kalettes to the skillet with the sautéed garlic. Pour the creamy sauce over the kalettes and mix well, cooking for another few minutes to let the flavors marry forever.

Grease a casserole dish with Vegan Compound #13 and transfer the creamy kalette mixture to it, using a spatula to flatten the kalettes into the sauce so it settles nicely into it in the thinnest layer you can get it.

Bakefor ~20-25 minutes and that's it, let cool before serving.

Tangy Coleslaw

½ bag (~8 oz) pre-shredded cabbage slaw mix
2 tbsp Dijon mustard
2 tbsp apple cider vinegar
2 tbsp extra virgin olive oil
1-2 tbsp lemon or even lime juice
1-2 tbsp stevia or monk fruit, to taste
Salt and pepper to taste
1 tsp celery seed (optional, for added oomph)

Makes 2-4 servings (depends on how slaw-hungry you are).

Place the pre-shredded cabbage slaw mix in a large mixing bowl.

In a separate mixing bowl, whisk together the olive oil, Dijon mustard, apple cider vinegar, lemon or even lime juice, and sweetener, salt and peppering tastefully (just like my goatee). If using the celery seed, add it now or forever hold your peace.

Pour the dressing over the shredded cabbage slaw mix and toss everything together until the cabbage is evenly coated with the tangy dressing.

This slaw works great as a side dish, protein bed or taco topping.

Creamy Coleslaw

A bag of coleslaw (~1 lb)
1 large (or 2 small) ripe avocado
½ cup silken tofu
2 tbsp lemon juice
2 tbsp apple cider vinegar
3 garlic cloves
2 tbsp Dijon mustard
Salt and pepper to taste
1 packet of stevia or monk fruit
2-3 tbsp water (adjust for desired consistency)

Makes 6 servings.

Combine all ingredients (except for the dry coleslaw) into a blender, press the Decimate button and bring it all to a smooth consistency, thickening it with more avocado or thinning it with more water as needed, while sweetening and salt and peppering to taste.

Place the shredded coleslaw into a mixing bowl, and pour the contents from the blender onto it, tossing to coat each individual veggie shred with the dressing. Voila, good to go!

Pickled Veggie Mandala

Pickled:
Asparagus
Artichoke hearts
Olives
Mushrooms
Yellow squash
Pickles
Kimchi

Makes 1 serving.

From your collection of pickled vegetables (see the discussion above in the Pantry Stocking section), arrange them sequentially in a circular pattern around a large dish, using the dish size to constrain portion sizes.

In Sanskrit, a 'mandala' is a circle that is used in ritual practices involving repetition and spiritual forms of focus. In the context of this dietary practice, regularly creating mandalas of your pickled vegetables aids with mindfulness, intentionality and routine, keeping you centered in a plant-based diet. For the veggie-only version of this recipe, leave the center of the dish empty as a symbol of primordial emptiness, which itself is a symbol of hunger. The first recipe in the next section adds a protein core to your pickled veggie mandala, if an empty center is not your thing. As noted above in the Meal Plan for Weight Loss section, this makes for a great first meal of the day.

Some pickled vegetables are quite high in carbs, such as carrots, peas and beets. These are not suggested for those with weight loss goals, and are more suitable for weight maintenance. This is a lot of food! I often cannot finish a whole plate. When I've eaten all I can, I cover the plate and then snack away at it throughout the day.

Simple Fancy Salad #1

Salad:
1 head of organic living (roots attached) butter lettuce
2 mini cucumbers

Dressing:
1 tbsp herb-flavored extra virgin olive oil (for example, Tuscan, Provençal or Milanese Gremolata herbs)
1 tbsp flavored white balsamic vinegar (for example, grapefruit or other citrus)
1 heaping tsp of Dijon mustard

Other ingredients:
Grated vegan parmesan
Salt and pepper

Variations: try different greens or green combinations instead of the butter lettuce.

Makes 1 large serving or several smaller ones.

If you find a grocery that sells 'living butter lettuce' maybe you should keep shopping there for all your veggie needs, as that shows they have good taste in greens! Living lettuce is lettuce that is still alive, which is evidenced by having its root system still attached.

Now it is time to make the living lettuce come unalive, so cut off those roots and toss them into your green compost waste bin. Separate the lettuce leaves and wash them well, dry and place into a salad tossing bowl. Chop the mini cukes and also drop them into the salad tossing bowl.

In a separate small mixing bowl, combine the salad dressing ingredients. The dijon mustard acts as an emulsifier, helping to better blend the oil and vinegar. Douse the dressing onto the salad and toss well. Sprinkle the vegan parmesan cheese onto the dressing-coasted salad and toss a bit more, so that the cheesy particles stick well to everything. Salt and pepper to taste (and toss a bit more after doing so).

Then, eat! This salad is really easy to make and better than most of what you usually find in any restaurant. If you want to make a complete meal of the salad, consider topping with a protein, such as slices of the Marinated Cedar Baked Tofu or Whisky Barrel Plank Baked Seitan.

Simple Fancy Salad #2

<u>Salad:</u>
4 cups from a small box of pre-washed organic arugula
A small container of (around 25) 'mixed medley multicolored'
cherry tomatoes
Salt and pepper to taste

<u>Dressing:</u>
1 tbsp herb-flavored extra virgin olive oil (for example, Tuscan,
Provençal or Milanese Gremolata herbs)
1 tbsp flavored white balsamic vinegar (for example, orange
vanilla or other citrus)

<u>Croutons:</u>
Leftover bread crusts from 3 slices of low carb bread (for example,
what's left over after making the Lentil Paté Toast)
1 tbsp herb-flavored extra virgin olive oil (for example, Tuscan,
Provençal or Milanese Gremolata herbs)
Grated vegan parmesan cheese
Salt and pepper to taste

Variations: try different greens or green combinations instead of
the arugula.

Makes 2 servings.

In some ways, this salad is a little less fancy than #1, omitting the
grated cheese and the use of Dijon mustard as an emulsifier and
going with a more straightforward oil and vinegar dressing.
However, this salad is a bit more fancy because it has croutons!

To make the croutons, take the crusts from 3 slices of low carb
bread and slice them into cubes. Place them in a mixing bowl and
add the flavored oil, tossing to coat them thoroughly. Salt and
pepper to taste. Sprinkle with the vegan parmesan cheese to taste
(or to your dietary goals) and toss a bit more. Place on a
parchment paper lined baking sheet, spread out evenly, and bake
for ~20 minutes at 350°F/177°C (adjust timing for desired level of

crispiness—they will be quite brown, since bread crusts are being used, especially if they are of a whole grain kind).

Slice each cherry tomato in half, to make them look more presentable (it just works, who knows why?). Place the arugula and tomatoes in a salad tossing bowl. In a separate small mixing bowl, whisk together the oil and vinegar. Add the dressing to the salad and toss well. Add salt and pepper to taste and toss a little more. Then, add the croutons and serve.

If you want to make a complete meal of the salad, consider topping with a protein, such as slices of the Marinated Cedar Baked Tofu or Whisky Barrel Plank Baked Seitan.

Caprese Salad

Technically tomatoes are a fruit but we associate salads with vegetables and so here it is with the salads. If this book had a section called "Fruit & Fat" for sure this dish would be there! This salad reminds you that the notion of "low carb" is quite relative, since vegan mozzarella can be a bit higher in carbs compared to most ingredients in this volume. And it's definitely not low fat! But in the scheme of things, compared to a Chicago deep dish pizza, this is a relatively healthy alternative. If your goals are weight loss, either skip the cheese (or use a lot less of it) or eat this on a cheat day, otherwise it is fine for caloric restriction and weight maintenance goals.

3 smallish or 2 medium sized tomatoes
1 tbsp herb flavored extra virgin olive oil
⅓ tbsp balsamic vinegar
Ball of vegan mozzarella cheese
Fresh oregano and basil (to taste)
Salt and pepper (to taste)

Makes 2 servings.

Cut the tomatoes and mozzarella ball into slices and place in a mixing bowl. You are generally looking for a similar number and size of cheese and tomato slices, for a visually well-balanced presentation. If you end up with extra cheese, set it aside for use later with the bruschetta recipe or another caprese.

In a small bowl, mix the oil and vinegar.

Separate the fresh oregano and basil from their stems and wash in a tea strainer (that's a great way to wash fresh herbs). Cut the basil leaves into smaller pieces because they are quite large compared to the oregano. You don't need too many fresh herbs but the more you throw into the salad, the more impressive it will look when photographing it :) and the flavor will pack more of an herbal punch (which sounds like an oxymoron).

Add the fresh herbs and oil vinegar mixture to the mixing bowl, toss with the cheese and tomato slices, and add salt and pepper to taste. Ready to serve!

Roasted Brown Cremini Mushrooms with Sage and Chives

1 pound brown cremini mushrooms, cleaned and halved
2 tbsp garlic or herb flavored extra virgin olive oil
1 tbsp minced garlic, with water squeezed out
8-10 fresh sage leaves, scissored
1 small handful of fresh chives, scissored
Salt and black pepper to taste

Makes 4 servings.

Preheat the oven to 400°F/205°C.

As a lazy cook, I am always seeking opportunities to take scissors to ingredients rather than chop them. Long straight chives stems and huge sage leaves are just perfect for cutting with scissors! So cut away.

Clean the cremini mushrooms and cut them in half, and toss with the olive oil and seasonings in a large tossing bowl. If you don't have a tossing bowl, a mixing bowl will also work. Make sure that the oil and seasonings are evenly coated with the mushrooms.

Salt and black pepper to taste and toss one more time.

Spread the seasoned mushrooms out in a single layer on a parchment-lined baking sheet, and roast for about 15-20 minutes or until the mushrooms look awesome (it sorta depends on how large your mushrooms are). If you're into opening oven doors and getting heat waves over your face, halfway through you can give it all a little stir to make the roasting more even. Personally, I am either a lazy cook, or I appreciate minor imperfections as part of my cooking aesthetic.

When serving, garnish with additional fresh chives and sage if desired. This will allow the discerning palette to make micro discriminations between fresh and roasted spices. If you find the taste of fresh sage as a garnish overpowering, just, you know, sprinkle some more salt and pepper on top!

Your kitchen, if not home, may smell like roasted chives and sage for hours, but that's cool.

Here's a tip: sauté a plant-based burger (one of the 'convenient proteins' discussed in the Pantry Stocking section). On the plate next to it, nestle these roasted mushrooms. Then, dump a big ladle of the Red Pepper Sauce from the Pasta section on top of both: this is a nifty and tasty fast meal!

Roasted Radishes

4 bunches of red radishes
1 tbsp avocado oil
salt, pepper, onion powder & garlic powder (to taste)

Makes 6 servings.

This is your low carb substitute for roasted baby potatoes!

Preheat the oven to 400°F/205°C (or if using a convection roast setting, 375°F/190°C).

Trim the greens and all the thin danglies off the radishes so that they are generally spherical, and wash thoroughly. Halve the radishes—some radishes may be much bigger than the others and need to be quartered. The radish pieces should be similar in size so that they cook the same—this is a very hard root vegetable so getting them all soft is important.

Place them in a large mixing bowl, add the oil and toss. Add the remaining spices to taste and toss some more. Spread them out evenly on a very large parchment paper lined baking sheet (I use a 16" x 24" / 40.5cm x 61cm sheet). Roast for 40 minutes (30 minutes if you want them more firm and less browned—I like mine soft!) and that's it, let cool and ready to serve.

These are great to leave in a bowl on the counter, next to a toothpick holder for day long snacking.

Boiled Chinese Mustard Greens

3 bunches Chinese Mustard Greens
1 tbsp sesame oil
1 tbsp soy sauce or tamari
1 tsp rice vinegar
1 tsp minced garlic, with water squeezed out
½ tsp minced ginger, with water squeezed out
Sesame seeds (optional)

Makes 2 servings.

Trim the ends of the Chinese Mustard Green bunches so that all the stems are separated, leaving you with very long pieces. Wash these thoroughly. Bring a large pot of water to a boil and add some salt to taste. Fill an adjacent large bowl with cold water for the ensuring shock treatment.

Place the greens into the pot and boil for ~2-3 minutes, making sure not to over-boil (the color will start to seem a bit depressing as it overcooks, so stop boiling if it starts to look a little sad).

Quickly dunk the greens into a large bowl of ice water or cold water to stop the cooking process—this helps retain its happy green color. You can make ice water by adding ice cubes to tap water.

In a small bowl, mix the sesame oil, tamari or soy sauce, rice vinegar, garlic and ginger. Adjust the ratios to taste. Remove the greens from the cold water, and pat them dry with paper towels. Transfer the greens to a large tossing bowl, then toss with the sauce until well coated. Add the sesame seeds into this tossing party if you go with that option. Ready to serve!

Cauliflower Buffalo Bombs

1 cup Buffalo sauce (see the recipe in the Proteins section)
4 cups of cauliflower florets thawed from frozen, or 1 head of cauliflower totally separated into florets
1 cup almond flour (or other low-carb flour)
1 cup unsweetened almond milk (or any non-dairy milk)
1 tsp garlic powder
1 tsp onion powder
½ tsp paprika
Salt and pepper to taste

Makes a plethora of small bite-size servings.

Variation: air fry instead of bake.

Preheat the oven to 425°F /218.333°C.

In a smallish mixing bowl, whisk together the almond flour, garlic powder, onion powder, paprika, salt and pepper until they are blended exactamundo. Then, add the almond (or other non-dairy) milk and whisk it all together again. Meet your batter! You have already met your Buffalo Sauce, because you made it first, following the recipe in the Protein section.

In a super massive mixing bowl (the kind that is very hard to find a place to store in your kitchen), dump the cauliflower florets. Because I'm lazy, I use thawed from frozen bags of florets, but you're welcome to start with a head of cauliflower and break it up into crumbly pieces that make a mess and add to the cleaning work.

Dump the batter-gloop onto the florets and stir softly, evenly coating each floret. Then, dump the buffalo sauce onto the batter glooped florets, and stir softly again.

With a very large slotted ladle or skimmer (so the excess glooped sauce can drip out of its bottom which is full of holes), scoop out the double-coated cauliflower florets and arrange them in a single layer on a baking sheet lined with parchment paper.

Bake for ~25 minutes and then check in on them. Open the oven door and say, "Hey what's up, little bombers?" That's just making conversation, though. You are actually checking to see when they're cooked fully and ready to eat.

Continue to check in on them every 5 minutes until they meet your cauliflower buffalo bomber expectations—the batter should start to get crispy but, you know, not burnt, etc. You can pour and brush on additional buffalo sauce if you want to increase your diet's intake of melted vegetable margarine, up to you ("Keto People in the House!"). Needless to say, the fat content of this dish makes it best as a cheat meal for those with weight loss goals.

Eat with toothpicks or even your fingers. Keep in mind that these are supposed to be a lot healthier than buffalo chicken wings ;~)

Caramelized Fennel

This recipe treads a *very* fine line between conceptual categories and distinctions such as Caramelized, Charred and Burnt. If you accidentally stray into Burnt territory, just tell your dinner guest(s) that the fennel has been charred 'in the Bulgarian manner.'

2 bulbs of fennel
2 tbsp herb-flavored extra virgin olive oil
2 tbsp fruit-flavored white balsamic vinegar
Salt and pepper to taste
2 tbsp additional cooking oil (avocado, olive, motor, tanker spilled, etc.)

Makes 4 servings.

Heat the cooking oil at medium low heat in a large skillet.

Thinly slice the fennel bulbs with a mandolin or V-slicer and place in a large mixing bowl. In a small mixing bowl, combine the oil and vinegar, then pour onto the fennel, tossing to coat it evenly white ambidextrously salt and peppering to taste.

Sautee the fennel in the skillet until it browns very darkly so that you can call it 'caramelized.' Ideally serve it with Egyptian Sprite (Sprite from a soda machine in Egypt) which is the best tasting Sprite in the world for some reason.

Otherwise, you can always just do a web search on "what goes well with caramelized fennel" since it has a rather pronounced licorice flavor (so, for example, do not pair with licorice).

Roasted Heirloom Carrots

2 bunches of small skinny heirloom (multicolorful) carrots
2 tbsp herb-flavored extra virgin olive oil
2 tbsp fruit-flavored white balsamic vinegar
1 tbsp dried herbs, consider Italian mix
Salt and pepper to taste

Makes 4 servings.

Preheat the oven to 400°F/205°C.

This recipe uses a similar flavoring mix as the caramelized fennel because the Mike Ludo diet is all about optimal laziness.

Trim both the green hairy and tiny pointy ends off the carrots, then wash thoroughly (and always wash all veggies thoroughly of course). Place the cleaned up carrots in a large mixing bowl, and drop the dried herbs onto them somewhat randomly and if I didn't know any better, as though you might be tipsy while cooking.

In a small mixing bowl, combine the oil and vinegar, then pour onto the carrots, tossing to coat them evenly. Salt and pepper to taste.

Spread the carrots out on a large baking sheet lined with parchment paper, and roast for ~1 hour or until they cry for help.

The dark purple carrots always look more 'burnt' compared to the other ones, so just go ahead and eat those yourself if others are afraid to.

Carrots have more sugar than most veggies in my low carb diet system, so if your goals are weight loss, reserve this dish for cheat meals.

Happy Baby Eggplant

This recipe takes its name from a yoga pose that is famous for making practitioners of that ancient art fart, or at least really want to while struggling to hold it in. Thus, this recipe is also a kind of homage to all new vegans whose gut biomes are adjusting!

It's also a great meal to start cooking in the slow cooker when you go to bed at night, since it takes ~8 hours even though you probably won't feel like eating baby eggplant for breakfast but who knows, you can always call it Morning Tagine! In which case, it does go well with low carb toast.

8 baby eggplants, quartered with ends trimmed off
1 can tomates broyées, ~800 ml
1 heaping tsp Italian mix dried herb
1 tsp onion powder
1 tsp garlic powder
1 tsp cumin
1 tsp paprika (Hungarian or Latvian or Smoked)
1 tbsp stevia or monk fruit
1 tbsp herb flavored extra virgin olive oil
Salt and pepper to taste

Makes 6 servings.

Tomates broyées is just French for crushed tomatoes, but in my head I imagine Keanu Reeves pronouncing it like "So Crates" in *Bill and Ted's Excellent Adventure*, in other words, Toe Mates.

Wash and trim the ends off the baby eggplant, then quarter them lengthwise. In a small slow cooker, add the crushed tomatoes and everything else except for the eggplant, and stir thoroughly. Then, add the eggplant.

Cook on low for ~8 hours while you are sleeping like a Happy Baby.

Lo Bak & Mini Bella Mushroom Pan Cake

Note that I call this recipe a 'pan cake' not a 'pancake' because it's just a kind of cake made in a pan, not the smaller stackable and flippable things usually served with syrup.

Trivia note: both veggies in this dish have two names! Lo bak is also called daikon (which you can lazily call 'huge white Chinese radish' or something) and mini bella mushrooms are also called brown cremini mushrooms.

1 bowl of the chickpea flatbread batter (see the recipe in the Bread section)
1 huge lo bak, peeled and grated
6 large mini bella mushrooms, finely chopped
2 tbsp minced garlic
2 tbsp herb flavored extra virgin olive oil

Makes 8 servings.

Make a batch of the chickpea flatbread batter, including its 30 minute rest time.

Heat the olive oil on a medium flame in a large deep skillet. If you heat it too low, it just takes *sooo loooong* to get all the water out of these wet veggies.

Peel and then grate the lo bak, which you will find is rather extraordinarily wet inside! Wow, is there a lot of water there, who knew?

Finely chop the mini bella mushrooms. I am usually too lazy to finely chop anything, so actually I just press it through a handy kitchen multi tool that includes a blade set to easily fine chop anything.

Saute the mushrooms and lo bak until all the water evaporates from both veggie entities— ~10-15 minutes—but before it completely evaporates, add in the minced garlic (garlic can overcook fast so it's a good idea to add it to the party a bit late).

Stir regularly, while salt and peppering to taste (remember that the chickpea batter also has some salt and pepper, so don't overdo it).

It's ok to admit that sauteing isn't always the most efficient way to get the water out of the pan and you may need to dump it all into a strainer a few times to get the water out, then resume cooking.

When the sauteed veggies are all looking pretty well dried out, cooked and exhausted, pour in the chickpea batter, give it a swirl, then cook with the cover askew (so some water can evaporate) at medium low for ~10 minutes. Now, you've got a cake cooked in a pan, which is why this is called a pan cake.

Note that the resulting dish has a consistency more like mashed potatoes mixed with hashbrowns, so don't expect it to act very cakelike beyond having chickpea flatbread batter to hold it all together like tasty legume mortar.

It is rather damn tasty and so doesn't really need hot sauce or any other condiment to go with.

If you find you like the idea, taste, experience and convenience of a batter based mash, check out the Failed Chocolate Chip Pancake Scramble in the Dessert section. This dish is better for cheat days for those with weight loss goals, because it's so addictive tasting, you'll probably end up eating the whole batch.

To get something a bit more cakelike out of this mix, after stirring the chickpea flour batter into the veggies, transfer it all to a parchment paper lined baking sheet, flatten it as thin as possible with a spatula, and bake at 400°F/205°C for ~15 minutes. This will get you a very moist and stuffed flatbread.

Seitan Sandwich Spread

The Mike Ludo food preparation methodology is always about optimizing taste and nutritional value against the parameters of time and laziness, and this recipe is no exception.
Seitan aka 'wheat meat' is a great sandwich filler but like all sandwiches, there is a need for other flavor components to make for a complete experience.
My go-to everyday seitan panini spread—I don't really make sandwiches unless they are grilled, as per my panini philosophy—is to combine all of the following into a small food processor, and store it in the fridge as an easy spread (use whatever proportions and ratios makes sense for your taste and machinery):

a handful of small olives
a handful of small pickles
4 heaping tbsp of dijon mustard
some revivified dried chilis (such as reawakened ancho chilis from my mole sauce recipe in the Proteins section)

A key advantage of a spread as opposed to other layered ingredients is that the sandwich will grill very nicely and evenly in a panini-maker, since if you have a bunch of other ingredients stacked in there with the seitan, the grill's heated surfaces may not evenly cover the whole (low carb of course) bread face.

Making a spread out of a number of flavor enhancing ingredients keeps the thickness of the sandwich manageable, makes it super easy to grill, and results in a rather flavorful and even photogenic panini outcome!

Protein + Veggies

Other dishes in this book also qualify as 'protein and veggies' but the other categories used are helpful for organization, so this section features protein and veggie combos that aren't also a Rice, a Chili, a Toast, a Pizza etc.

Egg Scramble

½ cup Egg Yolk Substitute (see the next recipe)
1 small onion, chopped
2 pasilla peppers, chopped
2 plum (roma) tomatoes, chopped
½ block soft tofu, ~225g, smashed (like, with a potato masher or equivalent)
4 soft boiled garlic cloves (optional, for garlic lovers only)
Seasoning to taste

Makes 2 servings.

Remember: soft and silken tofu are not the same thing! Silken tofu is used in the egg yolk substitute and is a great choice when you want a creamy result. Soft tofu holds its shape better and is more capable of chunkiness.

Remember: the egg yolk substitute is loaded with black salt, so you don't need to add salt to this dish! Dried herbs work well, though.

The psychology of this recipe is that the soft tofu is playing the part of egg whites, because it is white and protein based.

In a skillet, heat the oil at low heat, then add the smashed tofu, onion, pepper and tomatoes, stirring thoroughly. Add your chosen seasoning (dried herbs are great here). Cook until the onion and peppers are soft and the tomatoes stop crying, ~12-15 minutes, stirring occasionally.

If you're a garlic lover, add in the soft boiled garlic cloves around midway through, and smash them up with a spatula into the mix. A soft boiled garlic clove is just a garlic clove that has been boiled for 15 minutes until soft. I keep a container of these in my fridge at all times for emergency situations such as this egg scramble recipe.

Add in the egg yolk substitute, give it a nice stir, cook for a few more minutes then you're done. This scramble works great with two slices of low carb toast that have been brushed with a bit of oil while browning in the toaster oven.

Egg Yolk Substitute

This sauce uses principles of psychological subterfuge to make you not miss egg yolks. By using turmeric for yellow coloring and the sulfur in black salt, it provides a lot of the palette-pleasures of egg yolks—especially if warmed and treated as a sauce—though it doesn't try too hard to visually pass itself off as real egg yolk.

You can always close your eyes, if they insist that substances purporting to be egg yolkish should also look exactly the same as such.

1 cup silken tofu
4 tbsp nutritional yeast
1 teaspoon turmeric (for color)
1 teaspoon black salt (kala namak) for an eggy flavor (adjust to taste)
6 tbsp nondairy milk
1 tbsp extra virgin olive oil
A dash of black pepper (optional, to taste)

In a blender or food processor, combine all the ingredients until smooth and creamy. Thin with more nondairy milk if needed. Warm it up a bit, unless you've always loved room temperature egg yolk.

Use this in dishes where you could use a viscous liquid that sure tastes a lot like egg yolk. In the photo (medium.com/low-carb-vegan), this is used as a sauce to top the TVP Hash (in the Protein + Veggie section) which is my go-to breakfast meal.

Tacos w/ Soft Chickpea Shell

Makes ~6 *very filling* tacos plus extra flatbread remnants for miscellaneous uses.

This recipe is more simple than quick (especially if you make multiple fillings), but you can speed things up, and make it more fun, by making a team effort out of it.

Make the same batter as with the Chickpea Flatbread (Socca/Farinata) recipe in the Bread section, but double the ingredient amounts.

Preheat the oven to 450°F (230°C).

Line a large baking sheet with parchment paper and use a ladle to pour small circles of generally taco shell size (unfolded of course) across the baking sheet, leaving plenty of empty space around each flattened dollop. You will try very hard to get geometric circle shapes with the ladle that Pythagoras would be proud of, but you will ultimately fail, getting the batter just close enough.

Bake for ~15 minutes and there is your soft taco shell, just fold and stuff accordingly after it cools. The side facing the parchment paper will be wrinkly, so that should be the inside of the shell, and the top of each shell will be pretty smooth and work better as the outer shell.

Did I mention above in italics that these tacos are *very filling?* While inspired by Mexican street food—which is very popular here in Vancouver and elsewhere—I dare you to eat three or four of these in a row.

Feel free to buy a kitchen tool to get perfect circles out of the batter, if that concerns you, since there are always more tools you can buy which you don't own yet! The cooking aesthetic with this recipe is all about brutalist imperfections and that includes shape in this case, not just the texture.

Consider serving these tacos in colorful taco holders to impart a festive atmosphere or the sense that you went on an Amazon shopping spree.

Fillings Ideas

Classic

This one has three layers: shredded cheese on top of shredded lettuce on top of ground beef. Simply start at the bottom of the taco shell and layer up in the order of the fillings below.

Ground Beef Layer

2 cups rehydrated TVP
4-6 garlic cloves, chopped or minced
1 tbsp Spice blend (either Super Spice, described in the Pantry Stocking section, or taco blend, etc.)
2 tbsp avocado oil

Heat the avocado oil on low heat and add in the TVP and garlic, stirring to coat thoroughly with the oil. After ~5 minutes of sauteing and stirring, add the spice blend, sauteing and stirring for another ~5 minutes to marry the flavors without a prenup. Set aside and keep warm, as this is the bottom 'beef' layer of the classic taco.

Shredded Veggie Layer

2 cups coleslaw cabbage mix (dry, from bagged)
1 ½ tbsp chili flavored extra virgin olive oil
1 ½ tbsp orange (or other fruit) infused white balsamic vinegar
Juice from ½ lime
1 tbsp monk fruit or stevia (optional, for sweetness)
Small chopped tomato pieces (optional)

Place the slaw mix into a mixing bowl. In another small bowl, combine the olive oil and vinaigrette. Pour the oil and vinegar onto the slaw, add the lime juice and natural sweetener (if desired), and give a toss.

If your understanding of a classic taco is that there should be some tomato in there, adding a few small strategically placed pieces of tomato will suffice on top of the slaw mix.

Cheese Layer

1 tbsp shredded vegan cheddar cheese per taco

<u>Refried Beans Filling</u>

2 tbsp avocado oil
1 can of black soybeans (14 fl oz / 398 mL, easy to find on Amazon)
1 pasilla pepper, roughly chopped (just a couple big pieces)
2 serrano peppers
2 garlic cloves
2 little red chili peppers
1 cup brown cremini mushrooms, halved (optional)
Any prepared salsa

Heat a large skillet with the avocado oil at medium low heat.

Always after washing of course, slice off the stem sides of the peppers, split them in half and deseed.

Throw all of the above (except for the avocado oil and salsa) into a food processor and pulverize it all, then add to the skillet and saute for ~20 minutes, stirring occasionally and getting it into an overall refried bean shape. It will brown periodically which is nice, so stir to prevent over-browning and instead get that brown texture distributed evenly without it all going too dry. The mushroom is optional, as it will make the result softer and more moist, but also more flavorful, so up to you!

Set aside and keep warm, as this is the only component of the taco when serving. Top with a salsa of your choice.

Don't forget to always wash your hands after handling hot peppers, in case you casually rub your eyes later and experience a bit of what bears do when sprayed with aeresoled capsaicinoids.

Kimchi Tofu

1 ½ tbsp avocado oil
2 cups vegan kimchi
1 block of medium-to-firm tofu, ~170g

Heat the oil in a medium skillet at medium heat. Choose a kimchi with medium level spice to reinforce this sense of medium-ness.

Place the kimchi in a metal bowl and go at it with a scissors, snipping it to little pieces.

Cut the block of tofu into little pieces (you get to determine the tofu chunkiness).

Place both into the skillet, saute for ~10-15 minutes, stirring occasionally. Covering the skillet can speed up the self-steaming process. Saute until the kimchi loses its water or you can just strain it.

Magic Batter

There are at least three things that are magical about Magic Batter:

1: Anything goes! Or at least, anything that can go into a food processor :)
2: Thus, you get to draw on the magic of your imagination—what will you create with the great freedom and latitude afforded by ye olde food processor contraption?
3: So long as you put great ingredients into it, it will do magic for your body's health and well-being.

Magic Batter is this book's vegan mystery meat, in other words, a combo of protein and veggie matter that you can do meatloafy things with, like, well, make meatloaf, air fried meatballs, stuffed peppers filling, or shape into a pattie and sauté for burger delivery format (geometric integrity willing), and so on.

Below is a list of the ingredients I have included in the example of Magic Batter (and the resultant Meatloaf) that you can see online at medium.com/low-carb-vegan.

2 cans of black soy beans
Cooked riced cauliflower
Cooked broccoli florets
Dash of vegan Worcestershire sauce
8 whole garlic cloves
1 can of pitted black olives
A few pickles
2 cups of small pickled onions (note it will add some sourness, though)
5 shiitake mushrooms
A chunk of eggplant
2 serrano peppers
2 slotted spoons of capers
3 tbsp of Super Spice (see the recipe earlier in this book, in the Pantry Stocking section)

Makes many servings!

You can think of this as a bit like the idea of 'eating the colors of the rainbow' — as is often recommended of fruits and vegetables—only in this case, brown isn't really a color of the spectrum (though astronomers say that the average color of the universe is a kind of dark brown—go figure).

All of this—EXCEPT for the Super Spice and riced cauliflower— had to be run through my 2L food processor in two batches. Needless to say, ratios and measured amounts aren't too important here, since you are getting to make the clay that you will also sculpt your meal out of. See, it's that magical :)

Line a large baking sheet with cheesecloth or flour sack towels, and place the batter (as much as will fit—you may need to do this in multiple passes) in the center. Then, fold up the corners to wrap the raw batter inside it, so it looks like a baby in a stork package, and squeeze hard. This step is to expel as much water as possible from the batter, so that it has a more meat-like consistency after baking. Squeeze hard, to make it as dry as possible.

The harder you squeeze, the more water will come out, so let your first Magic Batter meatloaf motivated you to squeeze harder on your second batch ;~) You will then add this squeezed batter to the riced cauliflower, add the Super Spice (or any spices and herbs to your delight), and stir very very vigorously to make a uniform substance.

The two most essential ingredients of Magic Batter are the black soy beans, since those provide the complete protein (which justifies this substance being used as a mystery meat substitute), and the riced cauliflower, which helps the batter obtain some semblance of geometric shape and stability, allowing the cooked form to not collapse under its weight by providing some structural integrity, just as rice does in regular meatloaf.

You can use the occasion of creating Magic Batter as an opportunity to go through your pantry and fridge to see what can be thrown into it. Is it about to go bad? Throw it into the Magic Batter!

With the exception of the super spice and cooked riced cauliflower (which should be placed in a very large mixing bowl), run your ingredients through the food processor in any order that makes sense to you. Be mindful of the relationship between the amount of material your casserole dish (or stuffed peppers, etc.) can hold, relative to the size of your food processor, and adjust all ratios and portion sizes accordingly. I always use 2 cans of black soy beans, just to make sure I have a respectable amount of complete protein in the batter.

<u>Simple Batter Variation</u>
A more straightforward batter can be made just with:

Black soy beans
Cooked riced cauliflower
Onions
Garlic (cloves or minced)
Dried herbs and spices to taste

Follow the same steps as above.

Meatloaf

Magic Batter
Avocado oil

Makes many servings!

Preheat the oven to 400°F/205°C. Rub a large casserole dish with avocado oil for anti-stick purposes. Scoop the completed Magic Batter (with the riced cauliflower and spiced) into it, and bake uncovered—to let excess water evaporate—for 60-90 minutes. The exact timing will depend on how deep you have made your meatloaf, but this range will generally suffice.

Unlike regular meatloaf, this one is a completely balanced meal, due to all the veggies pre-combined with the protein. What you pair it with will be, well, magical! Hot sauce is a great choice.

Stuffed Peppers

Green bell peppers (as many as you wish to make)
Onions, any kind you like, chopped
TVP (textured vegetable protein)
Marinara sauce (see the recipe in the Pasta section)
Grated or shredded vegan cheese (optional, to taste)
Minced garlic, with water squeezed out, to taste
Herbs, spices, salt and pepper to taste
Flavored extra virgin olive oil

Variation: make the pepper filling out of the Magic Batter

Remember that green bell peppers have the lowest carb content of the bell pepper family, in case you are tempted by all the other colors they come in.

Preheat the oven to 400°F/205°C.

Surprise, green peppers come in irregular shapes and sizes, so this recipe requires some on-site assessment of spatial volumes and geometries. You want to hand select green peppers at the produce bin, making sure that the ones you pick have relatively flat bottoms so that they do not tip over or lean into each other when baking them.

Dehydrate the TVP according to the instructions on the package. The dehydrated TVP is the main stuffing for your peppers, so you'll have to eyeball how much TVP to rehydrate to fill your peppers. Err on the side of rehydrating more than you'll need, because you can always use the leftover TVP in the Bolognese sauce (see the recipe in the Pasta section), or in the TVP hash, or anything, really.

Sauté chopped onions in any flavored olive oil you prefer. Don't cook all the way to soft and translucent, because they will cook some more when baking the peppers. Add in the minced garlic and any combination of herbs, spices, salt and pepper to taste that you prefer. Stir well, then mix in the dehydrated TVP.

Keep a balance of flavored cooked onions and TVP in the stuffing blend, so that it makes the kind of filling you want in your peppers. Mix in some of the marinara sauce to get some tomato flavor prevalent throughout the filling. You can also add some grated or shredded vegan cheese into the stuffing if you want more saturated fat in your diet.

Scoop your mixture into cavernous insides of the bell peppers, which have had their tops sliced off, insides gutted, and of course—been washed thoroughly—in preparation for being stuffed. Brush the outsides of the peppers with the olive oil.

Rub a large casserole dish with avocado oil for anti-stick purposes. Place the stuffed peppers inside and bake uncovered for 45 minutes in total. 30 minutes into baking, brush the tops of each pepper with the marinara sauce for some color and taste pizazz.

Pickled Veggie Mandala with Protein Core

Create a pickled veggie mandala, as described in the previous Veggies section (the first recipe there). In the center of the plate, place a protein of your choice. The photo for this meal (see the Protein + Veggies page at medium.com/low-carb-vegan) shows a plant-based burger in the middle of the plate, topped with hot sauce, but you can place any protein there that suits you, such as sautéed marinated tofu strips or vegan sausage links . As noted above in the Meal Plan for Weight Loss, this makes for a great breakfast.

And this is a lot of food! I often cannot finish a whole plate. When I've eaten all I can, I cover the plate and then snack away at it throughout the day.

Makes 1 large serving.

Kimchi and Tofu

6 Marinated tofu slices
2 cups kimchi
1 tbsp extra virgin olive (or other vegetable) oil

Makes 1 serving.

With scissors, cut the kimchi into smaller pieces and sauté for 10-15 minutes at low heat (or high simmer) in any desired oil. Garlic-flavored olive oil works well, as will many others. Covering the kimchi will make it even softer when done.

In a separate small skillet, sauté the marinated tofu slices, which ideally will have been marinated overnight (I like spicy, and so often marinate my tofu in green chili flavored olive oil).

Move the sautéed kimchi onto a dish and just lay the tofu slices on top, that's it! Then practice your chopstick skills.

The Marco Polo

It looks like a panini but eats like a lasagna—the Marco Polo bridges the Mediterranean and classical Far East with its globe trotting logic. Or is it an illogic?

Two slices of eggplant
Herb-flavored extra virgin olive oil
Fresh thyme
1 tsp any low carb pesto
Vegan feta cheese block
3 slices of grilled marinated tofu (see the Marinated Tofu Slices recipe in the Protein section)

With a mandolin at the thicker (versus thinner) setting, cut into an eggplant lengthwise until you get two decent sandwich-sized slices. Conversely, with the mandolin at the thinner setting, cut a slice of the vegan cheese. This is because, as a metaphorical sandwich, it would just be odd if the cheese in the middle were thicker than the bread slices!

On the outer edges of the eggplant (the eggplant slices are the 'bread' of this sandwich), brush the olive oil. On the inside, layer with the thyme, pesto, cheese and tofu. Wrap in wax paper or parchment paper and grill for 15 minutes. Skip or go easy on the cheese if your goals are weight loss.

Experimental Charcuterie

½ cup marinated seitan
1 tbsp marmite
¼ cup sliced pickles
1½ tbsp honey
2 tbsp dijon mustard
2 slices of low carb bread
¾ cup vegan cheese slices (half white, half yellow)
1 tbsp balsamic vinegar
1 tbsp extra virgin olive oil
5 olives

Variation: substitute thicker baked seitan slices for thinner marmite-boiled seitan pieces.

Refer to the photo at medium.com/low-carb-vegan on the Protein and Veggies page.

Slice the seitan as thin as you can get it, for instance by running it through a mandolin at the thinnest setting. Slice the pickle similarly.

Cut the crusts off the bread, making neat squares or rectangles out of the slices, and toast them. Reserve the bread crust pieces for the croutons or dipping sticks discussed elsewhere in this book.

Lightly boil 3 cups of water in a small saucepan, and add the marmite to it, stirring so it dissolves. Add the seitan to the saucepan, reduce to a simmer, and let it simmer there for 30 minutes. The marmite will impart umami and salty flavors to the seitan, allowing you to pretend that it is like cured meats from Italy.

You can modulate the marmite flavor by experimenting with marinades for the seitan, or adding additional flavoring ingredients to the saucepan (experiment, since the recipe is called 'experimental' :)

Creatively arrange the pickles, seitan, vegan cheese slices, honey, mustard, olives, and bread on serving plates. The oil and vinegar should be on their own plate, for dipping the bread into.

Olives look cool next to a Polish crystal shot glass with toothpicks inside. And it goes without saying: eat this with wine if you drink wine.

The inclusion of honey and cheese should strongly suggest that this meal is better for a cheat day if you have weight loss goals. And charcuterie without honey and cheese, well, it just ain't.

TVP Zucchini Hash

2 tbsp extra virgin olive oil (a chili infusion in the oil will give a hint of heat)
1 medium zucchini— peeled and grated
1 medium onion—finely chopped
Dried herbs to taste (oregano and basil mix)
1 cup dehydrated TVP
Salt and pepper to taste

Variation: mixing in some leftover Caramelized Fennel, or the chopped stems from the fennel, adds interesting licorice flavor notes.

Makes 2 servings.

Rehydrate the TVP according to the instructions on the package. With TVP, it can be a bit difficult to gauge the amount to dehydrate relative to the actual amount you will end up using, so make a little extra as you can always find a use for any leftover dehydrated TVP since it easily takes the place of ground beef. If you end up with extra dehydrated TVP, see my TVP Ground Beef in Coffee recipe, which doesn't exist.

At medium low heat, sauté the onions, herbs, salt, pepper and rehydrated TVP, stirring occasionally, until the onions are halfway soft, ~10 minutes (depending on whether you are covering the pan to speed things up). Add the zucchini and keep stirring. Cover, turn up the heat, remove the lid occasionally to stir, then recover, and repeat for ~10 minutes.

This hash stubbornly refuses to change color as it cooks, so it can be a bit difficult to tell when it's done. Essentially, you'll get the feeling that the food is looking back up at you and telepathically says, "That's enough, now, we give up." You can confirm your cooking intuition by doing a little taste and checking for a ground beef hash type of experience.

Garnish with hot sauce. This is also a great regular breakfast for those with weight loss goals. Also consider smothering this in the Egg Yolk Substitute (see the recipe in the Protein + Veggies section) for extra nutritional yumminess.

Celtuce and Tofu Salad

If you've ever known someone named Julian, it's hard not to think about them when you julienne vegetables.

1 lettuce stem (celtuce), julienned
6 slices of the baked marinated tofu
1 tbsp tamari or soy sauce
1 tbsp sesame oil
1 tbsp rice vinegar
1 tsp minced garlic
½ tsp minced ginger
2 tbsp dried goji berries
½ tsp sesame seeds

Makes 1 large or 2 small servings.

Trim the ends of a celtuce (lettuce stem), and peel the hard skin off with a paring knife or robust peeler. Julienne it with a mandolin or mandolin—which is neither a Mandalorian nor a musical instrument—and transfer the thin shreds to a mixing bowl.

In a small mixing bowl, combine the oil, vinegar, soy or tamari, garlic and ginger, whisking it together with a fork.

Pour the dressing onto the celtuce, and toss along with the dried goji berries and sesame seeds. In a bowl, top or surround the salad with the tofu slices.

Pairs well with chopsticks.

Soups, Stews and Chilis

Kimchi Tofu Soup

2 cups kimchi
1 block of tofu, 350g
5 garlic cloves
1 cup vegan ground chorizo
1 green onion

Makes 4 servings.

Use scissors to cut up the kimchi into smaller pieces, and add to the soup pot. Cut the tofu block into cubes and add to the soup pot. Add 5 cups of water and the garlic cloves to the soup pot, turn on the heat and bring to a boil. Reduce to low heat and keep at a vigorous simmer for 30 minutes. Chop the green onion into small slivers and keep to the side. In the last 5 minutes, add the green onion slices and also the ground vegan chorizo, which replaces the ground pork that is often part of traditional kimchi tofu soup.

Seaweed Mushroom Soup

2 cups of Asian mushrooms (experiment! there are so many)
6 garlic cloves
1 tbsp sesame oil
2 tbsp soy sauce
1 cup cubed konjac (about half of a 250g block)
Chunk of ginger (about the size of a thumb joint)
1 green onion
A handful of dried nori (laver) seaweed

Makes 4 servings.

Chop the green onion into small slivers and set aside. Slice the mushrooms into whatever you consider to be a reasonable size for sliced mushrooms in a seaweed soup :) Slice the ginger chunk into ~6 thin slices.

Pour 6 cups of water into a large soup pot and add the sliced mushrooms, whole garlic cloves, sesame oil, soy sauce, cubed konjac and ginger. Bring to a boil, then reduce the heat to a high simmer for 20 minutes. Add in the handful of seaweed and green onions and simmer for another 10 minutes, then serve after a brief cooldown period.

The seaweed used here is *not* the thin sheets used to make sushi or kimbap. Rather, you are looking for a large rectangular package of a slab of unsalted seaweed, usually labeled 'laver' or 'nori' or both these plus also 'seaweed' (depending on the brand). See the photo at medium.com/low-carb-vegan on the 'Soups, Stews & Chilis' page for clarification if you are unfamiliar with this kind of seaweed. You want to just tear off a decent handful of the stuff to drop into the soup pot, and it cooks very quickly. Don't over-consume seaweed due to its high iodine content, which is not healthy for your thyroid functioning, but otherwise seaweed is very nutritious!

You shouldn't need any salt because of the soy sauce, but add it if you need more saltiness. Hopefully you know not to eat the ginger slices, which are just for flavor. On the other hand, the garlic cloves become very soft and are great to eat! And the cubed konjac makes this soup more filling then it would be otherwise.

Watercress Soup

Watercress is a rather unassuming superfood. On the shelves in the produce aisle, it doesn't stand out with deep colors or broad leaves. Usually, to be honest, it looks kinda sad, a bit small and damp with thin stems and tiny leaves. But put it under a microscope or analyze it with a Star Trek tricorder, and its nutritional profile of vitamins A, C & K, calcium and manganese, iron, phytonutrients and antioxidants makes you wonder why you haven't been eating or drinking watercress all your life!

1 tbsp avocado oil
1 tbsp herb flavored extra virgin olive oil (such as Tuscan, Milanese Gremolata or Provençal)
1 large onion, chopped
2 cups mushrooms (any kind, experiment!), sliced
1 tbsp minced garlic
half a 250g block of konjac, cubed
2 bunches of stem trimmed watercress

Trim the stems off the bottom of the watercress, and wash thoroughly. Usually with watercress you treat the greens differently depending on whether the stems are thick or thin, but since the soup will end up in the blender, at this stage you're just removing the stems at the cut side of the bunch.

Heat 6 cups of water in a kettle (you can vary this amount depending on how thick you want your soup). Bring the water to a boil and then turn off the kettle.

In a very large deep sauté pan, add the oils (if you only have one cooking oil available, just double the amount), onion, mushrooms, konjac cubes and cook at low (or high simmer) heat for ~10 minutes, stirring occasionally. Add the garlic and sauté for another 5 minutes or so, stirring until the onions are soft. Turn off the heat, then add the hot water, and stir the watercress into it.

Since you have to be very careful when you pour a large amount of very hot liquid into a blender, wait until the soup cools in the pan. Because large deep sauté pans usually lack pouring spouts, as an intermediate step I transfer the contents while they are still warm to a large mixing bowl I have that does have a pouring spout, and then from there I transfer all the contents into a very large (2.5 liter) blender, where all the contents are blended.

The soup is now ready to eat. The konjac makes the soup a lot more filling than it would be otherwise.

Chowder

4 cups thawed frozen cauliflower florets
1 cup chopped celery
1 medium-sized chopped onion
1 tbsp minced garlic
4 cups vegetable broth
1 cup unsweetened cashew milk
2 tbsp garlic or herbal (Tuscan, Milanese or Provençal) flavored extra virgin olive oil
½ tbsp fresh thyme
½ tbsp fresh rosemary
Salt and pepper to taste
½ cup nutritional yeast (optional but yummy, thank you heat-killed saccharomyces cerevisiae)
Fresh parsley for garnish

Makes 4 servings, or 1 very large extremely selfish one.

Remove the excess water from the minced garlic using my patented Squeeze It In Your Fist method.

If you only have large onions around, you can convert any large onion into a medium sized one simply by removing the outer layers until it can no longer be categorized as a 'large' onion. If you only have small onions around, 2 small = 1 medium sized onion.

In a large soup pot (note that you cannot convert a large soup pot into a medium one in the same way), heat the olive oil over medium low heat. Add the chopped onions and a few minutes later, add the minced garlic since garlic cooks faster than onion. Sauté both until nicély softénéd but not too softénéd.

Add the cauliflower and celery to the pot. Stir and cook for ~5-7 minutes until these new chopped vegetables begin to soften. Covering, uncovering, stirring, repeat will speed up the process a bit as the veggies steam themselves unwittingly.

Add the thyme, rosemary, salt, and pepper, stirring to coat everything with the new spices. Stir a few times and then add the vegetable broth.

Bring to a simmer, which will likely mean turning up the heat to precisely Low or Medium or Medium Low. If you are following my lazy cooking advice and using thawed-from-frozen cauliflower florets, it won't take as long for the cauliflower to become tender compared to starting with raw cauliflower. Simmer until pretty much everything is soft and tender, ~15-20 minutes. Remember, we're making a chowder and there should be no hint of veggie crunchiness.

To bring out the chowder vibe, scoop out exactly ~1-2 cups, run through a blender and pour it back into the pot. The blended portion will make you think of cream, while the remaining unblended cauliflower will make you think of the potatoes you are not eating.

Add the cashew milk and simmer for another 5-7 minutes. Because the cashew milk will cool everything down, you have no choice but to increase the heat again to bring to a simmer unless you have all day. Adjust salt as needed. If you want a cheesier flavor, stir in the nutritional yeast mid-way through during this final simmering phase.

Ready to serve hot, but not as hot as a McDonald's coffee! Garnish with chopped fresh parsley. Traveling through Türkiye has taught me that you can never add too much parsley to anything, so consider really pouring it on in the Türkish style.

Take a selfie with your chowder wearing your finest Nantucket wool hat and fleece-lined flannel shirt.

Cauliflower Soup & 'Mashed Potatoes'

1 head of cauliflower
1 tbsp herb flavored extra virgin olive oil (Tuscan, Milanese Gremolata or Provençal)
1 leek
1 medium onion
9 soft boiled garlic cloves (see the recipe in the Veggies section), no more and no less
1 package silken tofu, ~400g
2 cups vegetable broth (keep additional broth in reserve)
1 cup nondairy milk
2 tbsp nutritional yeast
Salt and pepper to taste
Fresh parsley for garnish

Variation: to get the 'mashed potatoes' version of this dish, just use less liquid!

Go crazy moment: just before eating, stir in ¼ to ½ tsp of black truffle sauce, which will transport you away to another universe, just like a hot bubble bath with wine goblets at your side.

Bring a large pot of water to a boil, then place the whole head of (washed, of course) cauliflower in it until soft, ~20 minutes. Poking it nonviolently with a fork will let you know when it is soft. When it cools, break it up into the florets unless you really want ouchy fingers. It's ok to toss the thick dense stem or sacrifice it to the green bin composting gods.

Meanwhile next door, heat the oil in a skillet at medium heat, and saute the onion and leeks until soft, salt and peppering to taste.

In a blender, combine all the ingredients and liquify. Admittedly, this uses up a whole 2.5 liter blender in my kitchen. Pour into a pot on the stove at low (simmering) heat to warm it up, and add 1 or more cup (or more, you decide) of the reserve broth, stirring to adjust the consistency.

It's a good idea to use the same pot you initially boiled the cauliflower in—this way, the soup will experience déjà vu or even déjà rêvé.

If you want to see a volcanic type phenomenon where the soup surface forms thick exploding bubbles, spraying soup all over your stove or under the pot lid, just turn up the heat like in science lab class.

When serving, garnish with fresh parsley .

Broccoli Cheddar Soup

1 head of broccoli, chopped (or let's be honest, thawed from frozen broccoli florets ;)
1 small onion, diced
1 tbsp minced garlic, water squeezed out
½ tbsp dried oregano
1 medium-sized carrot or zucchini, peeled or not peeled, but definitely grated
3 cups vegetable broth
1 cup unsweetened almond milk (or any non-dairy milk)
½ cup nutritional yeast
1 tbsp extra virgin olive oil
1 tsp Dijon mustard
½ tsp turmeric dust
Salt and pepper to taste

Makes 4 servings.

In a large pot, heat the olive oil over medium low heat. Add diced onion and after a few minutes, add the minced garlic and dried oregano, and sauté until all have been softened.

Zucchini vs Carrot: carrots have more sugar, so you can opt for zucchini instead. However, zucchini is green, like broccoli, and so opt for carrots or yellow zucchini if you need more color contrast in your visual composition. You're the artist!

To peel or not to peel: you will have to decide whether you want to work a bit harder or be lazier. Don't feel bad if you decide to be carrot-lazy, since veggie skin has all kinds of nutrients you can Google. If you want to feel more like a French chef with Michelin accolades or even an Italian grandmother in a village on the slopes of Sardinia, then peel away! Whether you peel or don't peel, you still have to grate, because this recipe says so.

Remember that when any aspect of cooking starts to feel like repetitive work, treat it as Zen meditation and an opportunity to engage in No Mind or mindfulness or mantra séance or whatever. Remember that the keyboard shortcut for French vowels, as in séance, purée, sauté, café, voilà and à la mode, is something that they teach at Michelin chef school.

Add the chopped broccoli and grated carrot or zucchini to the pot. Sauté for another ~10 minutes until the new vegetables have joined in on the softening party. Covering the pot will help the veggies steam themselves into submission. Remember that sometimes when you add in a lot more veggies like this, you may have to turn up the heat a little bit to get everything cooking again, due to physics.

Season with the salt, pepper and turmeric, stirring well to coat everything with everything else.

Pour in vegetable broth and bring the mixture to a boil or at least a bubbling simmer. Reduce the heat to low, cover the pot, and simmer for another ~10 minutes or until all is very tender (but in a good way).

Assuming your blender is good to go for placing very hot items into it, put it all into a blender and pulverize the contents down into their molecular components via the rapidly spinning blades therein. If you're feeling iffy about the integrity of your plastic when it comes into contact with hot food, let the pot cool down a bit before blending.

In a small bowl, whisk together the nutritional yeast, Dijon mustard and almond milk. Pour this mixture into the blended soup, stirring well to combine.

Add more milk or broth if the consistency is too thin, and adjust seasonings to taste. Garnish with nutritional yeast sprinkled on top, to really bring out the faux vegan cheesiness.

Chili

Chili is usually made with beans and beans are notoriously high in carbs. However, black soy beans are very low carbs (they are pretty much as low as carbs go with beans) and so work well with low carb diets and also for vegan diets, as they provide a complete protein.

A block of vegan cheese, such as cheddar (optional)
2 cans (14 oz, 398ml) of black soy beans (I buy these on Amazon)
1 red onion, diced small
1 green pepper, diced small
3 tbsp tomato paste
3 tbsp minced garlic
2 tbsp avocado oil
1 very large (or 2 medium) serrano peppers
1 cup ground vegan chorizo
½ cup water

Makes 6 servings.

With the exception of the cheese, in a small (~2 liter) slow cooker, add all the above ingredients and stir. Then add the chili spice blend (to taste, 1-3 tbsp), a mix of:

garlic powder
paprika
hot cayenne
onion powder
cumin
allspice

My version of the spice blend is to use equal parts of all spices except for the cumin, which is 2-3 times the amount of the other spices. Cumin is a classic spice for chilis, and so this makes that flavor a bit more prominent.

Cook on the high setting for ~5 hours. The longer you cook, the softer everything becomes. It is hard to overcook food in a slow cooker, so find the timing that suits your taste. Once in the bowl, grate a bit of the vegan cheese on top, if desired, when ready to serve.

If you find the taste of black soy beans odd in a chili, you can always replace them with red kidney beans and freeze them for your cheat meals. Over time, try splitting black soy and red kidney beans half/half until you gradually get used to the different taste. I don't think it tastes that different, especially with all the spices used, but everyone's palette is different.

Breads

Viking Love Loaf

2 cups almond flour
1 cup ground flax seeds
½ cup psyllium husk powder
1 tsp baking powder
½ tsp salt
1½ cups warm water
3 tbsp herb flavored extra virgin olive oil
1 tbsp apple cider vinegar
1 tbsp garlic flavored extra virgin olive oil

Makes 8 servings unless you're a very hungry Viking.

Variation: Incorporate regional Viking herbs such as lovage, dill, juniper, thyme, nettle and wild garlic (to taste, and not all at once!). Keep in mind that Vikings were also steeped in trade and raids, and so they had access to other herbs and spices such as allspice, cinnamon, cloves and nutmeg. Imagine yourself as a Viking baker and get creative, horn helmet on head and herb-spice mixtures no one else eats.

Preheat the oven to 350°F (175°C).

Grease a small casserole dish with the garlic flavored extra virgin oil for anti-stick purposes. Bonus if you have a casserole dish shaped like a Viking boat.

In a mixing bowl, whisk together the almond flour, ground flax seeds, psyllium husk powder, baking powder, and salt.

Mix together the warm water, herb flavored olive oil and apple cider vinegar and add to the dry ingredients. Massage everything with your hands until a dough forms.

Allow the dough to rest for about 5-10 minutes.

Transfer the dough to the casserole dish and shape it into a Viking Love Loaf.

Bake for ~1 hour, checking to see if the loaf sounds hollow when tapped. Echo, echo. The exact cooking time is both inversely and conversely relational to the square of the thickness of your bread and the area of your casserole dish to the power of 10.

You're supposed to let the bread cool for a little bit before eating it, but dang, it's hard to resist cutting off a slice of bread straight out of the oven!

You can dip the bread in olive oil like a good Norman.

Chickpea Flatbread (Socca/Farinata)

1 cup chickpea flour
1 cup water
3 tbsp herb flavored extra virgin olive oil
1 tsp salt
1 tsp Super Spice (see the recipe in the Pantry Stocking section)
Salt and pepper to taste

Variation: you can top the flat bread with anything, like herbs, sliced olives, sun-dried tomatoes, etc. I suggest making it without toppings the first time, so you can get ideas of how it handles and what you can lay on top of the batter while it bakes. Because the batter is very thin, you may have the best luck with adding toppings after baking it halfway through.

Mix the dry and wet ingredients separately, then add the wet stuff to the dry stuff in a whisking bowl. Whisk it all together and get the batter to be as smooth and lump free as possible. When you see lumps forming in the batter, attack them with the whisk. If you keep getting some lumps despite your best whisking efforts, either accept them as a minor imperfection or enroll in Michelin chef school.

Let the batter rest for at least 30 minutes. You also need the rest after attacking all those batter lumps.

Preheat the oven to 450°F (230°C). Use a cast-iron skillet (seasoned, oil-baked etc.) if you have it. Otherwise, a baking sheet will work.

If using a cast-iron skillet, place it in the preheated oven for a few minutes to heat it up. Otherwise, just line a baking sheet with the parchment paper. By tilting the baking surface, you can thin it out more, or don't tilt it and let gravity alone determine the thickness.

Pour the batter into the hot iron skillet (oiled a bit if you're paranoid about the flat bread sticking) or onto the parchment paper lined baking sheet, spreading it evenly to form a thin layer. Bake in the preheated oven for about 12-15 minutes. The edges should be darker and crispier than the middle, but if you're cooking on parchment paper, the paper may puff up a bit from the hot air moving around in the oven and interfere with this edge-crispiness ideal. So, if you've been looking for an excuse to invest in iron cookware, this might be it!

Let cool then eat etc. Maybe dip it in some of the melted raw honeycomb discussed in the Dessert section (on a cheat day of course), or with the next batch, explore some savory toppings.

Savory Muffins

1 cup almond flour
¼ cup nutritional yeast (for a cheesy flavor)
1 tsp baking powder
½ tsp baking soda
½ tsp salt
1 tsp dried oregano
1 tsp dried thyme or basil
1 tsp garlic powder
½ tsp onion powder
½ tsp black pepper
1½ cups unsweetened almond milk or any plant-based milk
¼ cup garlic or herb flavored extra virgin olive oil or for keto
fiends, melted coconut oil
1 tbsp apple cider vinegar
Sesame seeds (optional, for topping)
2-4 tbsp Grated vegan parmesan cheese (optional, for batter)

Makes 8 muffins.

Variation #1: see the chocolate chip muffin version in the Dessert section.

Variation #2: sauté some rehydrated TVP and add it into the batter to add protein and a ground beef vibe, which will also increase the number of muffins produced in proportion to the added TVP .

Variation #3: use the pulp-based 'dough' described in the Pizza section, just add spices and/or the sautéd TVP and bake directly.

Preheat the oven to 350°F/180°C. Grease a muffin/cupcake pan or line it with cupcake liners or get the cool pliable silicone cupcake sheet that lets you pop them up (but still grease those a bit).

In a large mixing bowl, whisk the almond flour, nutritional yeast, baking powder, salt, oregano, thyme or basil, garlic powder and black pepper. Add the grated vegan parmesan if desired.

In a separate bowl, mix the almond milk, olive oil and apple cider vinegar. Let this mix sit for a minute or so for the chemical chain reactions to initiate.

Pour the wet into the dry ingredients and stir until well combined.

Spoon the batter into the muffin/cupcake cups, filling each about ⅔. Smooth the tops with a flat spoon.

Sprinkle sesame seeds on top if you want them to seem seedy.

Bake for ~30-40 minutes or until the tops are golden brown and a toothpick inserted into the center comes out cleaner than when it went in (if you think about it, this makes sense, due to muffin friction).

Let cool for ~5 minutes before eating.

Chickpea Crepe Pancakes

These cook very fast on account of their thinness, so don't get distracted staring at your cellphone while these are a' griddlin' unless your middle name is Burnt.

These are so light, you definitely won't feel pregnant and sleepy after eating a plate, as you would with traditional pancakes.

1 cup chickpea flour
⅛ cup stevia or monk fruit
1 cup water
3 tbsp extra virgin olive oil
Coconut flower nectar (as a topping and using restraint)

Variation: instead of a syrup topping, consider a more French take using fresh squeezed lemon juice and sprinkled stevia or monk fruit.

Makes 7 smallish pancakes, which for me is like 1 serving :)

Mix the dry and wet ingredients separately (not including the coconut flower syrup), then add the wet stuff to the dry stuff in a mixing bowl. Whisk it all together and get the batter to be as smooth and lump-free as possible.

Let the batter rest for at least 30 minutes.

Heat some additional cooking oil in a skillet at medium heat, and ladle in the batter in smallish pancake-sized giant dollops. The batter is *very* runny and so a little goes a long way, perhaps ½ or ⅓ ladle per pancake. They will also be very thin, like crepes. When you see bubbles forming in the heated batter, flip the cake over so that both sides are treated equitably.

For syrup, you're in luck! Obtain some coconut flower nectar which is remarkably low in carbs compared to maple syrup and has a much lower glycemic index as well. Yum….

Savory Cobbler

Since I don't have a 'bread and veggies' category, a coin toss has determined that this recipe goes here with the breads instead of with the veggies.

2 cups almond flour
1 tbsp garlic powder
2 tbsp dried herbs, Italian mix
1 tsp paprika
1 tsp baking powder
1 cup water
5 tbsp herb flavored extra virgin olive oil for the batter (Tuscan, Milanese Gremolata or Provençal), 2 tbsp for sauteing the veggies and 3 tbsp for making the batter
1 large onion, chopped
8 large brown cremini mushrooms, chopped
1 leek, chopped (trim and discard the two less edible ends)
2 green bell peppers, chopped
2-3 tbsp minced garlic

Salt and pepper to taste

Make the flax eggs and let sit for 5 minutes.

Heat the 2 tbsp of herb flavored olive oil in a large skillet at medium low heat. Add the chopped mushrooms, onion, green peppers and leek, along with 1 tbsp of the dried Italian herbs, sauteing them covered until soft, ~20 minutes, stirring ocassionally. Salt and pepper to taste. Halfway to soft, add in the minced garlic.

Preheat the oven to 350°F/177°C.

In a large mixing bowl, stir to combine the almond flour, garlic powder, the remaining 1 tbsp of the dried herbs, paprika and baking powder. In a separate small mixing bowl, combine the 3 tbsp of herb flavored olive oil and 1 cup of nondairy milk. Add the wet mix and the flax eggs to the dry mix in the large mixing bowl. Whisk it all together to get the batter as smooth and lump-free as possible.

Grease a casserole dish. Pour the veggies in first, then top with the batter. Bake uncovered for ~1 hour. Let it cool before eating.

Snacks

Unsalted Mixed Nuts

A handful of mixed unsalted nuts is a great low carb vegan snack! This is not so much a recipe as a reminder :) Another reminder: not too many handfuls, or too large a handful…..(there are a lot of calories and fat grams there, after all).

Dried Fruits

With dried fruits, it can be easy to get perhaps a bit too much sugar, because you're basically eating miniaturized fruits and so the sugar in the large fruit is now compacted in much less volume.

In the context of a low carb diet, I find that dried fruits are mainly helpful after exercise, if I'm feeling a bit light headed and need a fast restoration to regular energy levels. Runners and cyclists, amongst others, have coined the term 'bonking' to describe the feeling of having run out of the body's glycogen and 'hitting a wall' where they can't go any further. Dried fruits can be thought of, then, as a 'fast debonker.'

It might be a good idea to hide them—like, find some dark inconvenient top shelf corner at the back of the panty— so they are not in easy reach. This way, you only resort to them when you need a healthy sugar hit.

Baked Tofu Slices & Soft Boiled Garlic Cloves

This is a super handy snack based on ingredients used throughout this cookbook. Just keep some baked marinated tofu slices (see the Protein section) on one fridge container, and in another fridge container, keep some soft boiled garlic cloves (see the recipe in the Veggies section).

As a simple healthy snack, just place a couple garlic cloves on top of a slice of the tofu, which can be remarkably addictive.

Chicharrón Prensado (konjac 'pork rind pressed')

Half a 250g block of konjac
Chili (or other hot spiced) flavored extra virgin olive oil
Salt: a specialty South American salt is cool, such as Andean Pink Salt or Bolivian Rose (to taste)

Makes 1-2 servings.

There is a Latin American variation of pork rinds that are soft rather than hard and crispy, which this dish imitates with the gelatinous slivers of konjac. You can almost think of this snack food as thicker gelatinous potato chips, if you find "Chicharrón Prensado" hard to remember :) With konjac, you can never say or write 'gelatinous' enough!

With a mandolin at the smallest setting, run the thin edge of the konjac block repeatedly across it, to create a mound of rectangular slivers. Sautée at low heat in the chili flavored olive oil, flipping over occasionally. You will see the konjac develop a nice pork rind reminiscent bubbly crunchy surface texture. And yet, it will refuse to get hard and crispy! Around the konjac slices, the oil will bubble up in interesting frothy ways as it interacts with the gelatinous substance.

When intuitively you feel you've sautéed the slivers long enough (about 15 minutes to my taste), place into a mixing bowl and toss with the salt to taste. Then, nibble away and lick your fingers as you do so.

This snack will satisfy a lot of the oil and salt cravings you might have with fresh made potato chips, only without the carb component. Needless to say, this is more of a weight maintenance or cheat day snack rather than a good idea for weight loss.

Toasted Bread Crust Sticks

Bread crusts from 3 slices of low carb bread (using math, that's 12 crust-lengths)
Extra virgin olive oil
Balsamic vinegar

Makes 1 serving

Take the bread crusts as is and place them on a parchment paper lined baking sheet, and bake at 350°F/177°C for 20 minutes (or longer, if you want them extra crisp).

On a separate plate, pour some olive oil and the vinegar, to be used for dipping the bread sticks into.

Exercise Fuel

Boiled Sweet Potatoes or Baked Japanese Purple Yams

As discussed in this book's introduction, sometimes you need more carbs to fuel more intense or longer duration exercise. An easy and healthy choice is boiled or baked potatoes, stored in the freezer for when you need them. I tend to make many of these at the same time, since I will be freezing them.

For boiled sweet potatoes, fill a large pot with as many of them as you can, covered in water and bring to a boil. Continue cooking them for 30 minutes (the longer you boil them, the lower their glycemic index value, but don't overcook them). When they cool, wrap them for freezing.

For baked Japanese purple yams (this kind is purple on the inside as well, not just purple on the skins as you find with other varieties—this is the same yam from Okinawa made famous by the Blue Zone diet), bake uncovered at 400°F/205°C for 60 minutes. When they cool, wrap for freezing.

Chickpea Flour Spirulina Keto Chip Cookies

As the song goes, 'so let's get down to business....'

Preheat the oven to 400°F (or 205°C).

Keep handy:
1 cup (or more, you decide) vegan keto chocolate chips (yes, these exist!)

In a larger bowl, whisk together the dry ingredients:
2 cups chickpea flour
1 tbsp baking powder
1/2 teaspoon salt
~1/2 cup Stevia
1 tablespoon of Spirulina

In a smaller bowl, whisk together the wet ingredients:
1 cup nondairy milk
1/4 cup vegetable oil (olive, grapeseed, avocado etc. all work fine)

In an even smaller bowl:
1 tablespoon Psyllium husks
2 tablespoon flax and chia seed blend
6 tablespoons of water (let these become gel-like)

Makes 5 big cookies.

Fold the wet and gelled ingredients into the dry ingredient bowl and mix them together into a batter and add in as many vegan keto chocolate chips as is reasonable.

Ladle your batter out into cookie-sized flattened dollops onto a baking sheet lined with parchment paper, and bake for 15 minutes. Let cool, then eat or freeze for cheat days etc.

Kohlrabi & Apple Semi-Sweet Casserole

1 large apple (nontart please)
1 kohlrabi bulb
Cinnamon for sprinkling to taste (consider Saigon Cinnamon because it sounds cool)
2 tbsp fruit infused white balsamic vinegar (consider orange vanilla)

Makes 8 servings.

Preheat the oven to 375°F/190°C.

Grease a small casserole dish with vegan Greasing Compound #2.

Like me—someone who is constantly bombarded by cyberstalkers and psychologically manipulative phishing and hacking attempts—kohlrabi bulbs have a very thick skin. However, removing that skin is a piece of cake, so long as your knives are sharp.

So, if your knife is a tad dull for the kohlrabi skin, sharpen it first, and then it will slice quite easily through it. Trim off the ends and slice away at the thick skin of the kohlrabi bulb until it is moist, naked and exhibits a strange random geometric shape due to your deskinning.

Run the moist naked bulb across a mandolin blade in order to get very thin slices of it. Place the kohlrabi slices aside, then run a large apple across the same mandolin blade to get thin slices of it. Because apples have seedy cores, you'll have to rotate the apple as you mandolin slice it, leaving a core to discard.

Pour the fruit flavored white balsamic vinegar into a small bowl, and keep a silicon brush handy.

In the casserole dish, lay a layer of kohlrabi slices just like you would the first layer of a lasagna, then brush it lightly on top with the vinegar. Then, layer on top of that a layer of the apple slices, and dust (or sprinkle) cinnamon on top of the apple layer.

Then, repeat the process: layering kohlrabi slices, brushing it with the fruit flavored vinegar, layering the apple slices, dusting it with the cinnamon, etc. until you are all out of kohlrabi and apple slices.

Bake covered for ~90 minutes until both kinds of veggie slices are soft, and you have yourself a nice semi-sweet casserole that is not quite a dessert nor yet a dinner or a side. It's more like a healthy sophisticated snack to pair with a nice sipping spirit, a single malt Scotch perhaps.

Drinks

Smoothed Spiced Coffee

1 pot of filter brewed coffee
1 tsp of cocoa and cinnamon blend (see the Spices section in
Pantry Stocking above)
Soy or almond milk (if desired)
Stevia or monk fruit (optional, sweeten to taste)

Special equipment needed: an Aeropress.

This is perhaps less a recipe than a hack :) What makes this coffee
'smoothed' is that I run filter brewed coffee through an Aeropress.
The microfiber filter in the Aeropress reduces the acidity of the
coffee (this is one of the unique features of the Aeropress
method).

Also, as you work your way down towards the bottom of a pot of
brewed coffee, the amount of fine coffee grains increases, making
for a rougher texture. The Aeropress will filter out these fine
grains of coffee that got past your coffee filter in the first pass.
Since grounds settle towards the bottom of a pot of brewed
coffee, more grains will be blocked by the Aeropress filter as you
progressively get towards the bottom of the pot.

The 'spiced' component to the recipe is to add a teaspoon of cocoa
and cinnamon blend, not so much to adulterate the pure coffee
connoisseur experience, but to obtain the health benefits of those
two spices. Add an unsweetened vegan milk, such as soy or
almond, if you like milky coffee. On your cheat days, consider
'going wild' with more sugary oat milk instead.

Fruit Sweetened Green Tea

Add a dollop of fruit-infused white balsamic vinegar to your unsweetened 0 calorie green tea and stir. The tea can be hot or cold, brewed yourself or pre-bottled. A light dollop of fruity white vinegar will go a long sweet way without adding a lot of calories. I like grapefruit and mango, but really anything will work, so explore flavors and experiment.

Simple Fancy Water

Add a few drops of (any desired) flavored white balsamic vinegar to water (water:vinegar ratio to taste).

This is one of those extremely minimalist recipes, if going strictly by word count!

Pizza Penance Juice

So, you've gone and done it, made some pulp-based pizza crust batter with raw cauliflower and broccoli. Well, you can atone for your pizza-loving ways by drinking the juice of your labors. If you find it's a bit too bitter to drink, just add stevia or monk fruit to taste, to sweeten the deal.

Pancake Penance Juice

So, you've gone and done it, made some pulp-based savory pancake batter with raw green bell peppers and zucchini. Well, you can atone for your pancake-loving ways by drinking the juice of your labors. Run this juice through a strainer to reduce the amount of froth and suspended particulate matter.

It should end up with a fluffy long lasting foamy head, like a good hefeweizen. If you find it's a bit too bitter to drink, just add stevia or monk fruit to taste, to sweeten the load.

Marijuana Wine

While initially wine may not seem to be a low carb beverage, think of it this way: adding some THC to your wine glass will pack enough mind altering punch so that one glass will suffice where normally you may drink much more! This is a calorie-efficient way of essentially squeezing a whole bottle's worth of partying into just one serving of respectably filled stemware.

Legally obtain cannabis oil, ideally a brand that comes with a syringe. Pour wine into a glass—either regular or non-alcoholic—and add the cannabis oil from the syringe into your wine, stirring gently. A full bodied wine works well because, hey, cannabis oil just makes the flavor more complex after all, bringing out the tannins or whatever. A fruity wine also works, since the slight bitterness of the oil gives the fruit something to fight against.

Contra 007, stir and not shake.

Desserts

Baked Apples

Apples (the exact number depends on how large your baking sheet is, and the type of apple depends on your tastes. For example, I personally don't like tart green apples much for baking)
Cinnamon (coat to taste)

You do NOT need to add sugar to get amazing baked apples!

With a handy apple coring and slicing tool, slice up a bunch of well-washed apples, and place the slices into a large mixing bowl. Sprinkle cinnamon generously, and toss well to evenly coat the apple slices with cinnamon. The more cinnamon you add, the more cinnamon you will taste!

Line a large baking sheet that has raised edges with parchment paper (mine can accommodate slices from a whole bag of apples). Evenly space out the slices on the parchment paper, then add some water to the baking sheet so that the slices are maybe a quarter submerged (this will help steam the apples). Cover with foil, and bake at 400°F/205°C for 1 hour. Let cool, then eat and store as is, or add them to the Whole Fruit and Nut/Seed Butter Toast described in the Toast section.

Sweetened Silken Tofu

1 cup silken tofu
1 tbsp (or less) mango flavored white balsamic vinegar

Makes 1 serving.

The dessert tofu you find in the stores is high in sugar. With this version, just take some silken tofu, add a fruit-flavored white balsamic vinegar, stir and eat. Mango is a very popular fruit for Asian desserts, but you can certainly experiment with other flavors.

Sliced Konjac with Mango Glaze

Speaking of mango:

5 slices (using a mandolin) of konjac
Mango flavored white balsamic vinegar

Makes 1 serving.

From a block of konjac, slice off as much as you want to eat (say, ~5 slices). Lightly brush the mango flavored vinegar, then practice your chopstick skills.

Fruit Quest

This 'recipe' is actually a fun shopping trip :) Identify the best place(s) in your area to buy the widest variety of fresh and/or organic fruits and vegetables. Since this is the Dessert section, our focus is on the fruits! At the store, scan the offerings for fruits you haven't had in a long time, or perhaps have never eaten at all. Logically, if you pursue this method, you will eventually cycle through all the fruits and then repeat the process. If you buy something you don't know how to eat, YouTube will teach you.

Buy enough fruits for 1-2 large plates, take home, wash and eat. Be aware of your allergies and of course don't eat anything you are allergic to (which also applies to every foot item in this book!).

If your goals are weight loss, this should be a cheat meal dessert, otherwise keep in mind the high amounts of simple sugars in fruits. Some do have significant carb content, such as bananas and plantains, but mainly fruit energy is sugar-based.

Frozen Fruit Purée

I rediscovered this dessert at a cafe in Lamu Old Town (on Kenya's east coast) when I got a strong sense of déjà vu while eating something very much like a soft mango ice cream. I used to make the exact same things years earlier in my first vegan phase in grad school. I looked over the counter of the cafe and sure enough, there was a Champion juicer, which is a true mechanical beast of heavy hardware. This device can purée frozen fruits (or vegetables I suppose, but who wants broccoli in a cold and soft format?).

If you have a juicer that can purée frozen fruits, then keep some ziplocked in your freezer for your cheat meals, either whole (like with strawberries) or chopped up (as with mangos). Your guide to frozen fruit chunk size should simply be the size of your juicer opening.

Just push the frozen fruit directly into the juicer with the right setting for this kind of work, and the purée will be the closest you can get to fruit flavored ice cream or sorbet or gelato or sherbet or frozen custard or granita or frozen yogurt or soft serve or melting popsicles with zero sugar or fat added.

Chocolate Chip Muffins à la Lava Mode

2 cups almond flour
½ (ore more!) cup keto vegan dark chocolate chips
½ cup stevia or monk fruit
½ tsp baking soda
Pinch of salt
½ cup unsweetened almond milk
2 flax eggs (2 tbsp ground flaxseed mixed with 5 tbsp water)
1 tsp vanilla extract

Makes 6 servings or you can think of it as 6 muffins.

Variation #1: make cookies out of the same batter, using cookie baking methodology.

Variation #2: make pancakes out of the same batter, using pancake cooking methodology.

Preheat the oven to 350°F /175°C and line a cupcake pan with muffin liners or grease one if not using liners (use Vegan Grease Compound #7). I really like the pliant silicone poppable kind of cupcake muffin tray.

In a large bowl, combine the almond flour, sweetener, baking soda and salt.

In a small bowl, prep the flax eggs by mixing the ground flaxseed with water. Let it sit for 5 minutes, then add the almond milk and vanilla extract. Stir well.

Gradually add the wet ingredients to the dry ingredients, stirring until well combined, then mix in the vegan keto chocolate chips. You may exceed the ½ cup threshold on the chips but only if you are prepared for more chocolate.

Stir and stir and stir and stir until every last single tiny batter lump has been abolished and the texture is as smooth as glass. This might require two days of stirring, but you will get there. Alternatively, accept a little lump of batter here and there.

Spoon the batter into the muffin containers, filling each about ¾ full and bake for no more or less than somewhere around 30 minutes, give or take a bunch of extra minutes, or until a toothpick inserted in the center comes out squeaky clean—oh wait, that doesn't work in this case. The issue arises that there are chocolate chips in this muffin, and in order for your toothpick to emerge clean, you would need Jedi level skills to deftly avoid any melted chocolate chips while piercing the muffin world. Good luck with that!

If your goal is weight loss, I wouldn't eat these for every meal, but more as something to enjoy once in a while as a cheat meal, to get a taste of what you *can* eat for every meal once you achieve your weight loss goals.

Right out of the oven, you can treat the muffins as 'molten' or 'lava' concoctions, as they are quite soft, and if you've loaded them up with keto vegan chocolate chips (is there any other kind?), they will totally deflate on a plate and you can serve it in hot molten lava dessert mode, proudly showing off how collapsed and hot they are. Once completely cooled off in the fridge, they will operate more as proper muffins.

Phyllo Fruit Pizza & Roll

Makes 8 servings.

Preheat the oven to 375°F/190°C.

Variation: before baking it, from one of the short edges, roll it up into a log and it will turn out more like a strudel or fruit carpet roll.

Follow the exact same steps as with preparing the phyllo layers as described in the Phyllo Dough Pizzas recipe in the Pizzas section, creating a well-brushed margarine or oil stack of 5-6 phyllo layers waiting to be topped. Or, you can save on calories by using cooking spray instead.

Run fresh or thawed from frozen fruit through a food processor. Pour the fruit slurry onto the top phyllo layer, and spread around with a brush. Bake for 15 minutes. The fruit will get *very* hot so let cool before eating. Eat it hand held or with a knife and fork, with the help of a pizza cutter of course.

This is best for a cheat meal or weight maintenance, given the sugar in the fruit.

Spiced Coconut Chocolate Cups

Get your keto vibe on with:

½ cup coconut oil, melted
½ cup cocoa powder (unsweetened)
¼ cup stevia or monk fruit
½ tbsp Super Spice (or to taste, see the recipe in the Pantry
Stocking section)
¼ tsp vanilla extract
Coconut flakes to taste
A pinch of salt

Get the ketonut, oops, I mean coconut oil into its liquid form,
which can be done various ways: for instance, have your dog lie on
top of a covered bowl of it, or gently irradiate it in the microwave,
or put it in a saucepan at barely visible flame height, etc. In
essence, it needs to be liquid and in a saucepan or mixing bowl,
and how you get there is up to you or even nobody's business. Add
the vanilla extract to the liquid coconut oil.

In another mixing bowl, combine the cocoa powder, sweetener,
Super Spice (or skip the spice if you want plain vanilla chocolate,
no pun intended) and a pinch of salt. Add this dry mixture slowly to
the liquid vanilla enhanced coconut oil. Stir well until the
ingredients are thoroughly combined.

Taste for the level of sweetness and spiciness you desire and
adjust accordingly. Add in the coconut flakes to taste—any
desirable amount is fine, really, so long as it makes sense—then
stir again to thoroughly mix the flakes into the liquid spiced
chocolate.

Pour the chocolate mixture into silicone molds or onto a
parchment-lined tray or into a container shaped like your dog or a
viking ship. Silicone molds are great for creating different shapes
so go wild. Or don't go wild.

Place inside the fridge where the chocolate will solidify, in an hour
or few. Keep these chilled and serve cold as the coconut oil will

start to melt in your fingers from your body heat, which makes these great fun to eat handheld or, um, body held. If you prefer less chocolate on your flesh, consider smaller sizes manipulated with toothpicks.

Eat on a cheat day or keto day or homemade chocolate day or toothpick day or finger licking day.

Raw Honeycomb

In my part of the world, I can obtain raw honeycomb by driving out into the rural areas and visiting the shops of the beekeepers, or I can drive five minutes down the road to a neighborhood Middle Eastern grocer. While not low carb per se, raw honeycomb is a great cheat meal dessert, and makes you feel exceptionally close to the food chain while developing empathy for struggling bee populations.

Raw honeycomb is basically sugar but with some amounts of trace elements (vitamins and minerals), antioxidants, enzymes (like amylase and invertase), and a resinous substance called propolis. The research on raw honey—and honeycomb—is pretty thin at the time of writing, but in general honey interests researchers and nutritionists for potential benefits related to wound healing, anti-inflammatory and antioxidant properties, immune system support, antibacterial and antimicrobial properties, and oral health.

While there may be some possible health benefits that can accrue from occasionally eating raw honeycomb, really you should just eat it because it's a natural source of great tasting and interesting to contemplate sticky energy. Consider pairing it with nuts and dried fruit, if you are particularly hungry!

When eating raw honeycomb, I sometimes find I get these chewy waxy pieces I really don't feel like chewing on any longer and swallowing. If eating alone, I politely cover my mouth with a table napkin and push it out of my mouth into a paper tissue. If eating with others in a social setting, I just put my fingers into my mouth and dig around to force it out and flick it onto the edge of my plate.

Phyllo Fruit Roll

5-6 layers of phyllo dough
1 ziplock bag of frozen fruit (~2-3 cups worth)

Preheat the oven to 375°F/190°C (sometime during the next step).

Run your chosen frozen fruit through a blender to pulverize it into little frozen fruit pebbles.

Use the Cooking Spray Phyllo Crust method discussed in the Pizza section. Start to make the Fruit Pizza described in this section, by laying out the frozen fruit pebbles evenly across the top layer of phyllo.

Before placing it in the oven, roll it up just like a carpet roll, or the Burek or Pizza Roll described earlier in this book. Then bake for 15 minutes and that's all she wrote bob's your uncle finito.

Unlike the phyllo pizzas or pizza roll or burek, the fruit roll—like the fruit pizza—is really too hot to handle when right out of the oven, due to the very hot fruit juice. This needs to cool down to room or fridge temperature before it is manageable to eat.

Gooey Sushi

This sweet treat is fun and sticky! Like, *really* sticky, which just makes it more fun.

Essentially, you want to take a balsamic reduction beyond the sauce state of matter usually aimed for, and reduce to thicken it until it cools into a balsamic goo.

Then, just spoon and stretch atop a slice of raw honeycomb, and you have a rather unique dessert concept that can only be called Gooey Sushi!

Raw honeycomb, ~400g
1 cup balsamic vinegar (lowest carb option you can find
3 tbsp monk fruit or stevia
½ tsp Dijon mustard (optional, for added flavor)
Pinch of salt

Makes a dozen gooey sushi bites.

In a small saucepan, combine the balsamic vinegar and low-carb sweetener. Add the pinch of salt. Place the saucepan over medium heat and bring the mixture to a simmer. Stir occasionally to dissolve the sweetener.

Once it starts simmering, reduce the heat to low to maintain a gentle simmer. Simmer the mixture for ~25 minutes. Stir occasionally to prevent burning. At some magical moment, it will suddenly froth up into a thick bubbly foam and you know you're getting somewhere!

If you like, add the Dijon mustard to during the last few minutes of simmering for an extra layer of flavor. Stir well.

Once it thickens into solid goo, lay a viscous dollop upon an unsuspecting sushi-sized slice of raw honeycomb, and serve it as gooey sushi to test everyon'e chopstick dexterity.

Do expect the cleanup to be a little tricky when the food is this sticky :)

Fruit and Chocolate Cobbler

2 cups almond flour
¼ cup stevia or monk fruit
1 tsp baking powder
1 cup nondairy milk
2 flax eggs (2 tbsp ground flaxseed mixed with 5 tbsp water)
4 tbsp extra virgin olive or avocado oil
1 tsp vanilla extract
½ cup vegan keto chocolate chips
4 cups mixed berries (thawed from frozen works well)

Preheat the oven to 350°F/177°C.

Make the flax eggs and let sit for 5 minutes.

In a large mixing bowl, stir to combine the almond flour, sweetener (stevia or monk fruit) and baking powder. In a separate small mixing bowl, combine the oil, vanilla extract and water. Add the flax eggs and wet mix to the dry mix in the large mixing bowl. Whisk it all together to get the batter as smooth and lump-free as possible.

Grease a casserole dish. Add in the fruit first and top with the batter, then sprinkle the vegan keto chocolate chips on top. If using large fruit like strawberries, cut them up with scissors to smaller pieces. If using thawed from frozen fruits, drain any excess liquid before adding to the casserole dish.

Bake uncovered for ~45 minutes. Let it cool before indulging.

If your dietary goals are weight loss, this is great for cheat days.

Failed Chocolate Chip Pancake Scramble

Sometimes you make a pancake batter that tastes really great but just completely fails to hold its shape as a pancake. Not to worry! Just throw all the batter into a skillet and scramble it like eggs, then eat it like a hot pudding or something :) It actually tastes far better than restaurant overpriced hot molten chocolate ganaches.

Needless to say, for those with weight loss ambitions, this meal is best for a cheat day.

1 cup almond flour
2 tbsp ground flaxseed
1 flax egg (2 tbsp ground flax + 5 tbsp water x 5 minutes to gel)
1 tsp baking powder
2 tbsp monk fruit or stevia
1/4 tsp salt
1 cup nondairy milk
1 tbsp extra virgin olive oil
1 cup vegan keto chocolate chips
1 tsp vanilla extract
Additional cooking oil or spray

Makes 4 servings.

Make the flax egg: In a small bowl, mix 2 tablespoons of ground flaxseed with 5 tablespoons of water. Let it sit for a few minutes until it thickens and forms a gel-like consistency.

In a larger mixing bowl, whisk together almond flour, ground flaxseed, baking powder, stevia or monk fruit, and salt.

To the dry ingredients, add the flax "egg," almond milk, extra virgin olive oil, and vanilla extract. Mix until well combined, then add in the vegan keto chocolate chips and stir once more.

Let the batter rest for 10 minutes.

Preheat a skillet or griddle over medium heat, and add the cooking oil or spray to make your cleanup work easier. When the skillet is heated, dump the batter in, stir it around the pan like scrambling eggs and cook for ~10 minutes, letting it thicken as moisture bubbles out of it. Periodically, scramble some more, and serve hot.

About the Author

Mike Ludo is the pen name of visual and musical artist Myk Eff whose alter ego is otherwise known in official real life as Michael Filimowicz, PhD. All three teach in the School of Interactive Arts and Technology at Simon Fraser University.

mikeludo.com
mykeff.com
michael-filimowicz.medium.com
twitter.com/myk_eff